ANGKOR

ANG

The Hidden Glories

A DAVID LARKIN BOOK

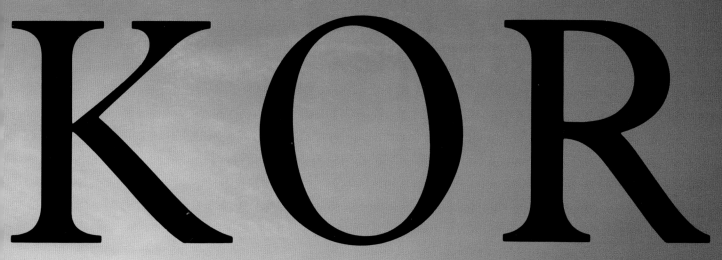

KOR

Michael Freeman and Roger Warner

Edited and designed by David Larkin

HOUGHTON MIFFLIN COMPANY   BOSTON   LONDON MELBOURNE

1990

For information about permission to reproduce selections
from this book, write to Permissions, Houghton Mifflin
Company, 2 Park Street, Boston, Massachusetts 02108.

Library of Congress Cataloging-in-Publication Data

Freeman, Michael.
    Angkor : the hidden glories / Michael Freeman,
Roger Warner.
        p.   cm.
    "A David Larkin book."
    Includes bibliographical references (p.256)
    ISBN 0-395-53757-6
    1. Angkor (City) — Description.   2. Angkor
(City) — Description — Views.   I. Warner, Roger.   II. Title.
DS554.98.A5F74   1990
959.6 — dc20   90-4828
                    CIP

Printed in Japan
DNP 10 9 8 7 6 5 4 3 2 1

CONTENTS

The Lost City

"With its millions of knotted limbs, the forest embraces the ruins with a violent love."

—ÉLIE FAURE, *Mon Périple*

We are riding in an old Russian Volga sedan, bumping along a dusty track before dawn. The headlights pick out the rutted holes in the road. We stop by a thatched lean-to for our guards, who carry Kalashnikov automatic rifles. We continue, and as the sky begins to lighten, we arrive at a stone gate tower with an eerie face carved at the top. A tree grows out of a crevice in the rock, in the center of its forehead. We are standing at the entrance to the temple of Ta Prohm, in the heart of the greatest complex of temples the world has ever known. This is Angkor, in the country now called Cambodia.

Ahead, a lightly worn path leads through waist-high grass; on either side is a wall of trees. There's a shout from behind, and one of the guards signals us to stop. He pushes past us and goes on ahead for a few yards, kneels, and does something that we can't quite make out in the dim light. He stands up and beckons us on. We learn that he has just disabled a tripwire connected to a small grenade in the bushes.

We reach an entrance in another wall, overgrown with creepers, and step carefully through the dark doorway. This opens onto a passageway that has partly collapsed. Our guides lead the way, turning into a side gallery before a wall of fallen stone blocks, turning again from passage to courtyard to passage, steering us through the maze. A bat sweeps past erratically, close enough for us to feel the movement of air; the sour smell of stale bat droppings fills the stone interior.

Near the center of the temple we stop in a courtyard. The jungle covers the walls; the corners of sandstone blocks poke out here and there between the leaves. Banyan trees grow right out of the walls, their roots like something out of a phantasmagoric dream—flowing down the walls like a liquid in slow motion, piercing the crevices with cunning precision, forcing the stones apart.

Overhead, the treetops are catching the first sunlight, and for a while there is silence in the surrounding forest. From the distance comes a descending series of notes, *HOO Hoo Hoo hoo hoo*, the call of a tropical dove. Silence follows, then far away there is a short burst of automatic gunfire. "Hunting birds," one of our guides says. We leave the guards and wander off.

Soon we are alone, feeling peaceful in the cool stone vaults. The stones press down on one another in their perfect fit. In nooks where nobody seems to have ventured for centuries, statues lie tumbled over in mossy repose. We come across a tablet incised in a strange, looping alphabet; we trace its letters with our fingers, as if somehow to unlock the mystery.

Passing through a doorway, we enter another courtyard. By the usual definition we are lost, but we have found what we are looking for. Carvings of gods and mythological serpents ornament every inch of the walls and the lintels. A young, tender vine has crept up the side of a voluptuous female spirit, or *apsara*. A strange feeling seizes us. Though we have flown into Cambodia and have driven in relative comfort from one temple to the next, there is something uncanny about exploring these overgrown ruins. It is as if we have discovered them for ourselves.

Of course, others have come before us. Among the first from a Western country was a young Frenchman, Henri Mouhot. He conceived of a plan—a fashionable pursuit in his day—to mount a one-man botanical expedition to the tropics and chose Southeast Asia as his destination, perhaps to prove his independence in his family's eyes. (A relative by marriage, the Englishman Mungo Park, was noted for his explorations of Africa.) In 1858 he left London for Bangkok and the following year took a boat along the northern coast of the Gulf of Siam to the Cambodian port of Kampot.

By January 1860 he had reached the town of Battambang, near the edge of a great freshwater lake, the Tonle Sap. A French missionary told him of the rumors of ancient ruins nearby and agreed to accompany him. Crossing the northwestern end of the lake, they could see a long mountain range in the distance, its peaks in the clouds. On the far shore they entered the mouth of a stream. Moving north, both by canoe and on foot through the dense forests, they finally reached a broad moat surrounding a temple. Mouhot stood on a raised stone platform from which a causeway crossed the moat to the main entrance. Directly ahead almost half a mile stood an immense stone building with five oddly shaped towers: the Temple of Angkor, Angkor Wat.

Mouhot did not know that he was looking at the largest religious monument in the world. He racked his imagination for comparisons in Western civilizations. Angkor Wat, he wrote later, was "a rival to [the temple] of Solomon, and erected by some ancient Michelangelo. . . . It is grander than anything left to us by Greece or Rome, and presents a sad contrast to the state of barbarism in which the nation is now plunged."

Mouhot spent three weeks in the Angkor region, taking measurements and making as complete an inventory as he could. He forgot about the original reason for his journey, collecting natural history specimens; the temples buried in the jungle were much more exciting. Ta Prohm, the site we came to more than a century and a quarter later, was just one of many to Mouhot; there were other temples on the same or a larger scale to explore. Angkor Wat, however, was the grandest of all. A shrine to which Buddhists made pilgrimages, it was in reasonable condition, but the rest of the ancient city had fared far less well.

More than two miles to the north he found that "a partly destroyed road, hidden by thick layers of sand and dust, and crossing a large ditch, half-filled with blocks of stone, portions of columns, and fragments of sculptured lions and elephants, leads to the gateway of

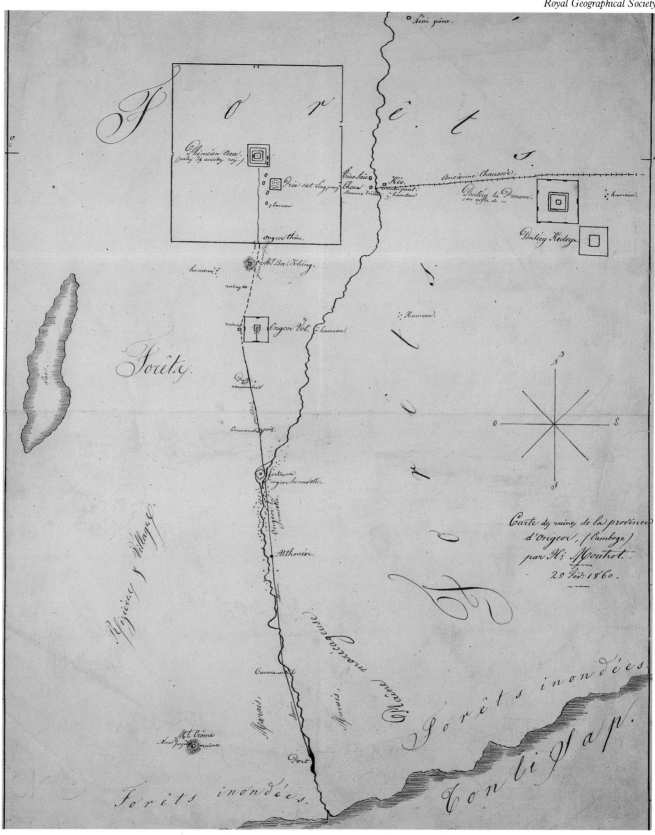

Henri Mouhot drew this sketch map in 1860, tracing his approach from the point where he disembarked on the Siem Reap River. Although sketched rather than surveyed, the basic elements are reasonably accurate, save for the misplacement of the Phimeanakas and the Bayon: the Phimeanakas is sited where the Bayon really is, and the latter is displaced to the east. These errors are excusable because of the lack of visibility inside the city; it was completely overgrown.

the town, which is built in the style of a triumphal arch." This arch breached a great wall of laterite blocks made from the hardened red earth characteristic of Southeast Asia. The wall enclosed what Mouhot estimated to be twenty-four square miles of almost impenetrable forest, broken here and there by overgrown ruins. Two miles beyond the gate was a huge mass of collapsed towers now known as the Bayon, then called "the hide-and-seek sanctuary" by the villagers. In this labyrinth of collapsed galleries, walls carried bas-reliefs with scenes from what appeared to be the city's history. There were views of court life, a naval battle, an army on the march, and more. But everything was in a state of collapse.

He wrote in his diary: "In numerous places the water, trickling through holes in the roof, has so obliterated the carving that the subjects can no longer be recognised." On every side the towers and gallery roofs were "intermingled with large trees, creepers and thistles, which invade the courts, the terraces, and other parts."

Mouhot sat on the top of Mount Bakheng, between the temple and the city, and looked out over the towers and the forest. "How many centuries and thousands of generations have passed away," he mused, "of which history, probably, will never tell us anything: what riches and treasures of art will remain for ever buried beneath these ruins." A romantic by temperament, he had found his own Ozymandias, a lost civilization, once great, about which no one knew anything. It was a desolate place, which also suited his romanticism. "All this region is now as lonely and deserted as formerly it must have been full of life and cheerfulness," Mouhot wrote. "The howling of wild animals, and the cries of a few birds, alone disturb the solitude."

Reports of Angkor's existence had been circulating before Mouhot's visit. An Englishman named Sir John Bowring had traveled in neighboring Siam in 1855, and he too had heard tales from French missionaries. In 1857 he reported, "Not far from Lake Thalesap [Tonle Sap] are the ruins of a vast palace, whose columns, pyramids and pagodas remain, sculptured in marble, of such elaborate workmanship, that the Cambodians boast they were produced by the fingers of gods, and not men."

There is no marble at Angkor—the carvings are in sandstone—and it is likely that Bowring never saw the place himself. In the year of his publication, however, another Englishman, D. O. King, explored near Angkor. In a lecture at London's Royal Geographical Society, King declared, "At the northern extremity of the lake in the vicinity of Simrap [Siem Reap] was situated the ancient capital of Cambodia, no trace of which now remains, except in the Nokon Temple, spared from destruction when the city was taken by the Cochin Chinese in about A.D. 200. . . . The temple stands solitary and alone in the jungle, in too perfect order to be called a ruin, a relic of a race far ahead of the present in all the arts and sciences."

King's talk attracted little attention. Near-oblivion was also the fate of a more thorough contemporaneous account by another Englishman, James Campbell, a naval surgeon based at the Bangkok consulate. Although he himself was not an explorer, he acquired the papers of a traveler named E. F. J. Forrest. Forrest had already died by the time Campbell read the manuscripts, and there is no record of when he might have reached Angkor. Nevertheless, as transcribed by Campbell, the detail is exact, down to the dimensions of the temple causeway.

"Standing alone in a country now depopulated," Campbell wrote, "and overgrown with forest wherein not even a house of the smallest description can be found constructed of stone, these ruins cannot fail to strike the beholder with the utmost wonder." Whether these are Forrest's words or Campbell's is not clear, but the writer goes on to express an opinion that became virtually an article of faith among everyone who followed, including Mouhot. The ruins "are indicative as they are of an age and people to whose vigour, power and talent the present debased and enervated condition of the Cambodian forms a most powerfully painful contrast."

Campbell presented his paper to the Royal Geographical Society, but it was neither read nor published. The glory of bringing Angkor to the public's attention, if not actually discovering it, went to Henri Mouhot, who, however, did not live long enough to enjoy his fame.

In late 1861, in the mountainous forests of Laos hundreds of miles up the Mekong River from Cambodia, Mouhot fell sick. He had counted himself fortunate to have kept his health until then. Nineteenth-century tropical medicine was inadequate; the European cemeteries in cities like Singapore and Saigon testified to the premature death of many of the colonists. On the nineteenth of October he wrote in his diary, "Attacked by fever." Ten days later he made his final entry, "Have pity on me, oh my God!" He died on the tenth of November. His servants buried him in the forest and returned to Bangkok with his possessions, including his diary.

This notebook, which eventually was returned to his wife, set off a remarkable train of events culminating in the exploration of Angkor and its restoration. In 1863 the diary appeared in installments in the French magazine *Tour du Monde*, and in the following year it was translated and published in English as a book. No doubt aided by the romantic circumstances of Mouhot's death, the account caught the imagination of Europe. Mouhot was credited with discovering Angkor, and the French lost no time in mounting additional expeditions. By 1878 major statues were on display in Paris, and in 1885 an archaeological inventory was started. A new era had begun for Angkor.

Cambodia was then being threatened by its two neighbors, Siam and Cochin China, each of which had annexed large parts of its territory. Cochin China ruled the area east of the Mekong River; Siam controlled much of western Cambodia, which included Angkor itself. But all that was about to change.

The French were caught up in a race with their rivals, the British, to exploit and colonize the Orient. Believing (erroneously, as it turned out) that the Mekong River would serve as a major route for trade with China, the French took Saigon in 1861, the year of Mouhot's death, and two years later persuaded Cambodia's King Norodom to make his country a French protectorate. Siam, to the west, was also being fought over by the British and the French, but it was in a position to negotiate and cleverly played the two European nations against each other. In return for abandoning its claim on the whole of Cambodia, Siam was allowed by the French to keep control for the time being over Battambang and Siem Reap provinces, which included Angkor.

But events didn't stop there. The French governor in Saigon decided to make an expedition to prove the Mekong's value as a trade route and to perform some imperial flag-waving. Included in the itinerary was Angkor, and the 1866 mission, led by Captain Doudart de Lagrée, was the first official expedition to the ruins. Louis Delaporte, a naval lieutenant on this expedition, then led a mission expressly to investigate the Khmer monuments in 1873—and incidentally to take some of the finest sculptures back to France.

French interest in Angkor grew concurrently with French colonial expansion. By 1887 de facto control of Cambodia passed to France, and by 1907 the Siamese had ceded back the western provinces. French archaeologists now had complete access to Angkor. The establishment of the École Française d'Extrême-Orient in 1898 put the exploration and restoration of the temples on a sound footing. It attracted a succession of scholars who devoted their considerable talents and energies to uncovering the glorious Khmer past. Through their work, they helped to restore not only the temples but also Khmer pride. The work of the French at Angkor became one of the few untarnished episodes in the modern history of Indochina.

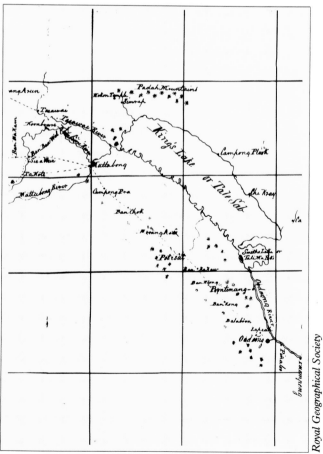

Royal Geographical Society

King's map

At the outset, the task seemed overwhelming. Only Angkor Wat was in any reasonable condition. Henri Parmentier, the leading archaeologist of the École, said of the Bayon, "Before work started, it was an incomprehensible maze, dangerous to explore, and all the more profoundly affecting and romantic." The same was true of almost all of the other temples.

The stones were scattered around the sites in no obvious order, and no surveys or ancient drawings existed to guide the reconstruction. Only painstaking study and labor over decades enabled the French and a cadre of Khmer workers to make a start. Some of the biggest projects, like the Baphuon, were hardly touched by the time the repercussions of the Vietnam War put an end to the entire effort.

Rebuilding was only part of the task, however. The scholars at the École also undertook the difficult job of determining who had built the cities and temples, and when. The Cambodians themselves were of little help. The ruins encouraged all kinds of superstition, and it was generally accepted in the region that Angkor could have been built only by angels or giants. Its scale was immense, the work involved prodigious, and yet, it had been abandoned for several hundred years, with no history linking it to modern times.

Among the French and other Europeans, the gap between ancient and modern fueled wonderful speculation. Perhaps the Romans built Angkor, they said. Or Alexander the Great. Or an ancient Indian race. Or even the Chinese. Mouhot thought Angkor probably dated from before the Christian era. No nineteenth-century European seriously imagined that the Cambodians built Angkor themselves. The idea of a lost great race overwhelmed by current barbarians suited the logic of these builders much better. It particularly suited the French *mission civilisatrice,* for by the time France had established the Union Indochinoise, its colonial administrators had formed the opinion that Cambodians were lazy and culturally decadent. The history of Angkor—or lack of it—was being written in European drawing rooms.

Indeed, many people wanted Angkor to remain a mystery. Fortunately, the best scholars of the École, based in Hanoi, took a more practical approach and began an inventory in 1879. From the start, they knew that the architecture and the carvings of Angkor owed much to India, but soon it became clear that the Buddhism practiced by the monks at Angkor Wat was not the religion that had inspired the motifs. Bas-relief carvings on the buildings showed Hindu gods, Vishnu and Siva in particular.

THAILAND

Bangkok
CAMBODIA
Angkor ■
VIETNAM

Phnom Penh

Ho Chi Minh City

Southeast Asia

Although debate over the dates and natures of the buildings raged for decades, most of the answers were settled definitively by the inscriptions. The most important were on free-standing stone slabs or stele—and not only at Angkor; stones were found as far away as Laos. The inscriptions were in either Sanskrit or the archaic form of the Cambodian language, old Khmer.

One by one, the inscriptions yielded to the patient French scholars. In addition to eulogies of kings, there were detailed descriptions of provisions and expenditures: accountants' ledgers of rice production, temple inventories, the numbers of priests, how much hemorrhoid salve was consumed annually by the hospitals, and so on. This kind of meticulous documentation was just what the epigraphers of the École needed in order to reconstruct the organization and the chronology of the Khmer empire. It became clear that the main construction took place from the end of the ninth century to the beginning of the thirteenth. To many it seemed incredible that all these monuments could have been built in less than four hundred years. Angkor's flowering had been brief but glorious.

Another myth—that of the palace—was laid to rest. Perhaps Sir John Bowring had created this illusion with his talk of a vast palace by the lake. The only remains were stone, and it seemed natural to assume that the kings lived in at least some of the buildings. The drawback was that few of the buildings actually seemed comfortable as dwelling places. Describing the dark, constricted interior of the Bayon, Campbell wrote that the small chambers leading from one to the other "could have afforded but scanty accommodation to the Royal occupants and their dependents."

In truth, they did not, for the stone ruins that concerned the French archaeologists were all religious monuments. The palaces and all the other secular buildings had been wooden and had long since completely perished. Not a trace remains of the structures themselves, but there is evidence of their appearance and construction. At the Bayon and in the terraces in the middle of the city, bas-reliefs show images of the surrounding wooden buildings. They have elaborate tiered roofs, supported by posts, that are pitched steeply and decorated heavily with finials.

Interestingly, the stone architecture contains echoes of the wooden buildings' construction details. Some of the sandstone door frames, for example, have mitered joints; they are structurally useless but perfectly understandable as an imitation of wood. Gallery roofs are sculpted with false tiles. Balustered windows imitate wooden ones that must have been turned on lathes. Before the builders of Angkor became stonemasons, they must certainly have been skilled carpenters.

The stone itself was not found in the immediate area but came from the Phnom Kulen, a long range of mountains some twenty miles to the northeast. A slightly bluish-gray sandstone, it was relatively easy to work and was thus a perfect material for the carvers and sculptors. Transporting it must have involved an enormous amount of manpower. When it was realized that the quantity of stone used in Angkor Wat alone was more than that in the great pyramid of Khafre in Egypt, the implications of the scale of the buildings became clear. To have been able to construct and maintain these temples, the Khmer society must have been not only efficiently, perhaps ruthlessly, organized but also very prosperous indeed.

Although the Khmers designed great architectural projects and were masters of decoration and sculpture, they were no engineers. One of the peculiarities of all the stone buildings at Angkor is that the Khmers seem never to have grasped the idea of the vault. They moved directly from building palaces of wood to temples of brick and stone without learning how to span large spaces.

The arch and the vault, which came later, are two basic features of building in stone: both direct the weight of the stone down onto the walls. They were first used by the ancient Egyptians and then developed

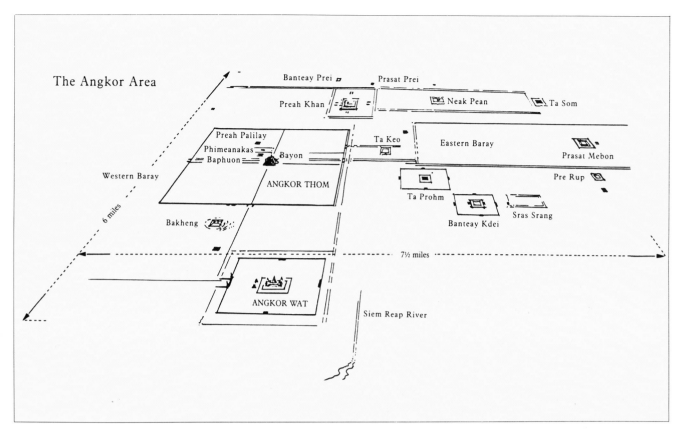

The Angkor Area

Banteay Prei
Prasat Prei
Preah Khan
Neak Pean
Ta Som
Preah Palilay
Phimeanakas
Baphuon
Bayon
Ta Keo
Eastern Baray
Prasat Mebon
Western Baray
ANGKOR THOM
Pre Rup
Ta Prohm
6 miles
Bakheng
Banteay Kdei
Sras Srang
7½ miles
ANGKOR WAT
Siem Reap River

by the Romans. With the flourishing of Gothic art in Europe in the twelfth century, religious architecture was dominated by engineers and the great cathedral naves were triumphs of vaulting. At the same time in Angkor, however, the architects were content to use the false vault, also known as corbeling. This meant that the workers first finished the walls and then laid a succession of blocks on top of them, making them reach inward as far as possible without caving in.

Eventually they did cave in, even though the entrances and corridors were quite narrow. The masons had failed to take obvious precautions. Instead of overlapping the vertical joints between one course of stones and the next, they often piled blocks on top of one another so that the joints ran straight down through the wall. As a result, in some places only one stone had to be dislodged for a whole section of wall to come crashing down.

This disintegration was the ultimate fate of all the temples save Angkor Wat. Abandoned for nearly five hundred years, they sagged and crumbled, helped from time to time by looters searching for treasure and bronze fittings. And, of course, they were assaulted by nature—by lichen and vines and, most spectacularly, by strangler fig or banyan trees, like those we saw in Ta Prohm.

Strangler figs are one of the most remarkable plant groups in the tropical forest. Their seeds, carried by birds, germinate far from the ground in tall trees or, as in Angkor, on the top of towers. The seeds send aerial roots down to the ground, hugging the stone for support, and they multiply and thicken until the stone structure is encased in a woody mesh. Some of the roots penetrate gaps in the masonry and over decades pry the stones apart, gradually breaking up the temple. At Ta Prohm, these trees were never cleared. They were deliberately left in place by the French archaeologists, as a manicured example of the ruins they had found to contrast with the extensive restoration elsewhere.

As we wander through the courtyards at Ta Prohm, we see Angkor much as Mouhot must have seen it, in the forest's embrace. Yet when we return several months later, the temple has been transformed. Laborers have been cutting vines and weeds with their *coup-coups* (machetes). The results leave us with mixed feelings. On the one hand, it is easier to perceive the intentions of those who built the temple. On the other hand, the temple seems bare. The experience of encountering the primeval has been lost. We tell ourselves not to worry. In just a blink of an eye on Angkor's time scale, the forest will return.

15

"It is difficult for someone who has not seen it to picture so wild and ramshackle a confusion of animate and inanimate, of rampant green life at war with immobile grey death, golden death. Indeed, the stone itself acquires a kind of life from the struggle, for it is caught between two fires, branches stretching upward and downward to destroy it, so that the architecture, obliged thus to take part in a battle, seems here to assume a dynamic, rather than its usual static, aspect."

Osbert Sitwell.

"With its millions of knotted limbs, the forest embraces the ruins with a violent love."

Élie Faure.

"The hardly recognisable debris of architecture poked out from everywhere, mingled with ferns, cycads, orchids, with all this flora of the eternal half-light that had spread under the vault of giant trees."

Pierre Loti.

In an engraving from Louis Delaporte's account of his 1873 expedition, one of the entrances to the temple of Preah Khan stands half ruined and overgrown. Although romantic in style, the view does not exaggerate. This remained the condition of many Khmer temples well into this century, of some even now. Pierre Loti wrote: "The fig tree rules as the master of Angkor today. Over the palace, over the temples which it has patiently broken up, everywhere it triumphantly extends its smooth pale branches, like the coils of a serpent, and its great dome of foliage. At first it was no more than a tiny seed carried by the wind onto a frieze or the top of a tower [in reality, more likely by a bird in its droppings]. But as soon as it could germinate its roots crept like fine threads between the stones, down, down, guided by a sure instinct toward the soil, and, when they finally reached it, they quickly swelled with the nourishing sap, until they had become enormous, forcing apart and unbalancing everything, splitting the walls from top to bottom. Defenceless, the building was lost."

Under the mat of green vegetation the powerful root of a *Ceiba pentandra*, the silk-cotton tree, embraces a sanctuary tower, forcing apart the sandstone blocks like a muscular arm. When the French naval commander Louis Delaporte led his expedition to this site in 1868, some of his sailors first thought that the giant roots in the shadows were serpents. The French archaeologists deliberately left these giant trees in place in Ta Prohm to show their destructive power. After the cities were abandoned in 1432, the jungle was quick to reclaim them—and still is. When the Khmer Rouge moved into the temples in 1971 as they prepared to take over the country, the care of the temples was once again abandoned to the forest, and after nearly two undisturbed decades, the vegetation has once more covered them.

"Crowned with high, pointed tiaras, dancers extend their fingers in the significant gestures of Cambodian ballet from mossy walls under cascades of green leaves or sprays of flowers," wrote Pierre Loti. Intended for the eyes of gods rather than men, this carving of a celestial maiden graces a hidden corridor just 3 feet wide in the maze of sanctuaries and chapels in Ta Prohm. One of the principal motifs in Khmer temples, *apsaras* like this one were the heavenly entertainers of the gods and their charms the rewards of kings and heroes. The delicate leaves of a creeper appear to decorate the figure; in fact, they are the first touch of the forest that, left alone, will eventually engulf the wall.

20

Leaves bedeck a carved stone floral frieze at the temple of Preah Khan. Although picturesque, the untended vegetation is ultimately destructive, and keeping the Angkor monuments in a state of order demands constant attention. Before the civil war of the 1970s, several hundred workers were employed by the Angkor Conservancy to tend, maintain, and repair the temples.

"A *fromager* surges a hundred feet up from the crest of a wall to reach the light and escape the green darkness; it has sent down to the soil a root as broad and full as a woman's breast, clinging tightly to the rock-face. Then, having reached the ground, it leaves the building to find nourishment among the broken stones 50 metres away." Using the French term for the silk-cotton or kapok tree, Élie Faure evoked the smothering impression of these destructive plants in *Mon Périple*. The roots of one tree follow a vaulted gallery roof before descending.

The other tree that swarms over the ruins at Angkor is the banyan-like strangler fig (*Ficus gibbosa*). Its roots are thinner and darker than the kapok's but no less pervasive. It starts life as an epiphyte, usually high in the fork of a tree or a stone tower. "Another, refusing to stray over empty space, frames a doorway and gallery perfectly with a torrent of tentacles. They stream around corniches and projections as if refusing to break them up." Élie Faure.

At Banteay Preah Khan, Louis Delaporte recorded the appearance of a causeway embellished with a row of *garudas,* the mythical half-man, half-bird. Élie Faure wrote: "The forest will not let the ruins escape. It bypasses the blocks, groping to find their moulded projections, decides to clutch them with hooks stronger than steel crampons. . . . The branches take on every kind of shape and function: hooks, forks, mortises, nuts, pulleys, stirrups, imposing a living organism that forces the worked stone to accept its embrace."

On a boundary post at Preah Khan, the woody stem of a creeper clings to the carved figure of a *garuda* with its clawlike tendrils, searching for crevices into which it can force its way—though here without success. If it does find a gap, it will eventually crack it open farther, although a creeper like this is by no means as dangerous as the powerful strangler fig. Over the foot of the *garuda* are termite corridors, at the lower left. Termites are an additional complication in the relationship between forest and monument. They consume dead wood and might have played a part in destroying wooden ceilings and reinforcing beams; however, the temples used relatively little wood. In the forest, termites attack the woody parts of dead plants, then turn them into a mulch for new growth.

". . . then Taprohm, under vegetation and trees in an atmosphere of decomposition and fever. The enormous white *fromagers* digest the stone embedded in their interconnected web, this root that covers and clasps a portico and comes to take the place of a pillar." Paul Claudel.

"Tree roots of huge, exaggerated size, bulky as a forest tree in northern latitudes, interpose themselves between the pillars of a cloister, cracking them as easily as a giant crushes a walnut with his hand, stone roofs are torn and twisted, and across some of the largest of them, even, straddle these tropical trees, bearing to them the same proportion as would an oak growing from a man's head." Osbert Sitwell.

Chaosay Tevoda, in the style of Angkor Wat though slightly earlier, lies a few hundred yards to the east of Angkor Thom's Victory Gate. A strangler fig, now fully grown to a tree, has almost destroyed the southern porch of the sanctuary. At the same time, however, its roots hold together many of the loosened stones.

The bright green patina covering the grimacing head of a *kala* over an entrance is a *Protococcus* algae, a sign of great dampness in the stone. The arrangement of the *fronton* stones above, or the trees higher still, channels water onto this area of carving when rain falls. The stone monuments are now known to be subject to a large variety of organisms and physical action, often making the diagnosis of damage complex.

Looking like a skin pigmentation disease, blotches of a crustose lichen grow on the face of one of the giant demons lining the causeway entrance to Angkor Thom. This damp-loving lichen grows in and on the substrata of the stone; when it dries it contracts, and it can have a constricting effect on the stone surface similar to that of dropping hot wax on human skin. If the stone is in good condition it may not be damaged, but if it is soft and friable, as much of the stone at Angkor is now, the decay can be accelerated. A special danger is vigorous cleaning without careful conservation research.

A victim of the collapse of a colonnade at the entrance
to the Bayon, a dancing *apsara* was disfigured when the
corner of a stone block struck its face. The colonnade
in its turn had been struck by a falling tree.

A sanctuary tower in Ta Prohm.

34

Laterite was available to the Khmers throughout most of the country. When it is quarried it is red and soft and can be easily cut into blocks; left in the sun to dry, it hardens to become structurally very strong. It is, however, almost impossible to work finely, and it was used mainly in foundations and enclosure walls.

The building material that the Khmers inherited from the earlier period of Cambodian history was brick, manufactured to a high standard. The vegetable binding used to lay bricks was very strong indeed, and completed walls were virtually solid blocks; often, where a wall has collapsed, the bricks themselves have split before the joints have come apart. Bas-reliefs like this figure in one of the towers of Prasat Kravan, east of Angkor Wat, were carved after the bricks had been laid.

Sandstone eventually became the principal building material for Khmer temples. At Angkor, most of the stone came from the Kulen plateau, some 20 miles to the northeast. The difficulties of transporting it and using it for construction—both a result of its weight—ultimately counted less than its permanence and its suitability for exquisitely detailed carving. In Takeo, the first temple built entirely of sandstone in about the year 1000, the massive blocks were left undecorated. The plain finish conveys some of the stone's best qualities: mass and precision (Khmer masonry was dressed for a perfect fit, and mortar was not used). A frieze surrounding the sanctuary at Phimai shows the delicacy that carvers could achieve with the relatively soft sandstone of the region.

Certain peculiarities in the ancient Khmer building methods hastened the collapse of the stone monuments after they were abandoned. Although the sandstone blocks were usually dressed with precision, the vertical joints were allowed to run on top of one another, making many of the walls inherently unstable. Often it took only one stone near the base to become dislodged to bring those above it crashing down, causing the collapse of a whole section of wall.

In contrast to the outer surfaces, the interiors of the temples are usually bare, leading to the speculation that they may originally have been decorated with murals. Here, in the central sanctuary of Preah Khan, holes in the walls suggest another possible decoration: bronze plates, which would have been an early target for looters.

A consequence of laying down the masonry courses without staggering the vertical joints was a gradual loosening of the construction. Mortar was not used; the builders relied on weight, gravity, and a good fit between the stones. Ultimately, with subsidence and the prizing effect of vegetation, the blocks began to separate.

Unlike Mediterranean and European builders, the Khmers never learned to use the arch. This failure not only limited their architecture in certain ways but also hastened the collapse of many buildings. Having first built in wood and then brick, the Khmers had structural difficulties when they came to use stone. The basic problem was the much greater weight of the new material, a factor that can actually help the stability of large buildings, but only if it is used in such a way that the loads are distributed properly.

The most efficient way of spanning two walls with stone is a curved arch, which conducts the load outward as well as downward to either side and so down to the ground. Vaulting, however, requires a knowledge of engineering and some precise mechanics, and the Khmers had no example to follow in the region. A second difficulty with vaulting is that until the roof is complete, with the keystone in place, it needs to be held up in some way, such as by means of a temporary framework or an earth support.

The Khmer solution was the false arch, also known as the corbeled arch. In this technique, massive stones are placed on top of each wall, one level at a time, projecting inward as far as possible without collapsing. It worked, after a fashion, but it prevented the Khmer builders from constructing wide galleries and entrances. This in turn influenced the architectural style; for instance, one way the Khmers achieved width was by adding a half gallery on one side, with columns separating it from the main gallery.

Recalling a Hindu dictum to the effect that only a corbeled vault sits quietly at rest, the French archaeologist and architect Henri Parmentier believed that the Khmers actually preferred not to use a true arch so that "the lie of the stone remains horizontal instead of converging towards a centre." However, there are too many signs that the corbeled vault was a restriction that the Khmers tried to overcome in different ways. The jutting interior edges of the blocks, for instance, were normally concealed by wooden ceilings and by decorative gable ends.

44

(preceding page)

"One tiny root, swelling little by little, has ruptured a wall and caused a vault to cave in. But at the same time it supports a carved stone where, after ten centuries, we can see the slow, swaying rhythm of dancing *apsaras*. It didn't want to let the stone fall, and cradles it in its arms like a mother."

Élie Faure

The ultimate result of corbeling, combined with other defects and all the pressures of nature, is the collapse of the vaults, leaving some of the galleries open to the sky and the forest—and so to more exposure to the elements and faster decay. In a gallery near the temple's foundation stele, part of the vaulting at Preah Khan has collapsed. In the passage beyond, the rough finish of the roof is typical of the way in which corbeled vaults were constructed. The necessary size and overlap of the corbels made it difficult to finish them attractively, and they were hidden by a lower wooden ceiling, long since perished. A further inducement for building a separate ceiling was the naturally somber appearance of the steeply pitched vault; structurally, there was no possibility of inserting windows to alleviate the gloom above.

Although some of the earliest explorers assumed that the monuments included palaces, it quickly became clear that they were all temples. Even the royal buildings were light wooden structures, long since disappeared. Our clearest view of secular Khmer architecture is presented in bas-relief carvings, such as this panel on one of the Baphuon's pavilion walls, from about 1060. An open structure of posts and beams, its most distinctive feature is its steeply pitched roof, with sweeping gable ends and embellished with ridge finials. Two centuries later, a Chinese emissary wrote that "the tiles of the central dwelling are of lead; other parts of the palace are covered with pottery tiles, yellow in colour."

This style, little changed in the centuries since, is still characteristic of modern Cambodia, Thailand, and Laos, although it is now confined to temple architecture.

An echo can also be found in the stone monuments of Angkor itself. On a gallery roof at Angkor Wat, the common clay tiles are faithfully imitated in stone, at considerable effort for the carver.

(preceding page)

Broken walls now let in more light than would ever have reached the stone galleries of the temple of Ta Prohm. Most of the massive square columns, however, have held up. Resembling the posts in the carved stone picture of a wooden building, Khmer columns and capitals were not elaborated by the masons, in contrast to those of Greece and Rome. Nevertheless, like the Doric and Ionic orders, they were derived directly from wooden architecture. The capital performs the same function as its wooden counterpart: it spreads the load from the beams above. The door frame contains another imitation of carpentry: the joints at the corners are mitered.

The laboriously carved stone balusters, so typical of Khmer temple windows, were undoubtedly modeled on lathe-turned wooden originals. All of these, which would probably have decorated the palaces and dwellings of the king and upper echelons of the hierarchy, have long since rotted back into the forest, but the legacy remains. Near the northwestern limit of the empire, in what is now northern Thailand, the window of a teak temple hall in Chiangmai shows exactly the same form. Even the gilding and small mirrors on either side, a common feature, may have a precedent. An account of the palace at Angkor from the end of the thirteenth century describes "a golden window, with mirrors disposed on square columns to the right and left of the window-trim, forty or so in number."

The recently restored inner enclosure wall of the temple of Phnom Rung, a little north of the Dangrek Range separating Cambodia from Thailand, clearly shows the continuous lines of the vertical joints, which can only have contributed to its earlier collapse.

The temple of Preah Ko, one of the earliest in the
plains north of the Great Lake, was completed in 879,
according to its foundation stele. Dedicated to the god
Siva, it consisted of six brick towers on a low, tiered
pyramid. The front three towers seen here each contained a statue of Siva; the three behind had statues of
the god's wife, Gauri. Originally, the brick was covered
with stucco decoration; only patches now remain.

The central group of sanctuaries of Banteay Kdei lies
some 2 miles east of the city walls of Angkor Thom. A
crowded collection of towers and connecting galleries
on a flat plain is surrounded by a galleried enclosure,
itself partly collapsed. No inscriptions were found describing its name or purpose; its modern name is derived from the site of an ancient village called Kuti.

Facing the sunrise, the towers of Pre Rup are once
again overgrown. Local superstition accounts for its
modern name, which means "turning the body"; it refers to a cremation ritual in which the outline of a body
is traced in the cinders one way and then the other.
There is no evidence to support this legend, however.
In the foreground, brick entrance lodges are connected
by a laterite wall enclosing almost 130,000 square feet.
The central towers, behind, stand on a tiered square
pyramid.

The Khmer Empire

"Having obtained supreme royalty in the holy city of Yasodharapura, after defeating the mass of his enemies, the king placed pillars commemorating his glory in all directions, as far as the sea."

—From the stele of Preah Khan at Angkor

"The kingdom possesses war-elephants to the number of 200,000."

62

It is another morning, and the fresh, sweet air has not yet surrendered to the sun's heat. We have just come out of Preah Ko, a group of towers built by an ancient king in honor of his mother. Behind us is the tinkling of ox bells; the peaceful beasts have been led to graze on the temple grounds to help keep the weeds down. At our feet lies a soft red laterite road. It has rained the night before, and the only prints in the dust are those of the oxen themselves. Preah Ko means "sacred ox" in Khmer.

To our right, the road follows a straight line south until it meets a transverse row of coconut palms. We look past the fronds of two tall palms leaning toward one another and see a ziggurat, a stone pyramid many stories high with a corncob tower on top. It is huge and old and perfect in a land that seems to have ancient temples in abundance. As we stare, Buddhist monks walk past the base of the temple, the orange of their robes seeming to glow.

Gradually we become aware of a soft commotion around us: roosters crowing, chicks cheeping, women talking. We in our transience and the temples in their permanence are in the midst of a village of *pilotis*, houses on tall wooden stilts. Turning to our left, we catch the eye of a housewife, who smiles shyly from her porch and raises both hands together in a graceful gesture called *sompeah*. Behind her are the sounds of water splashing and women laughing.

We walk over to investigate and find a rice field, divided by low earthen dikes into smaller plots or paddies. Two young women in sarongs stand in water up to their calves in a paddy used as a seed bed. The seedlings are now a foot high, luxuriant and crowded, and are ready to be transplanted to the rest of the field. The morning sun illuminates the green of the stalks from behind, like light coming through the stained glass of a cathedral.

With practiced motions, the women reach down for a handful of stalks, pull them up, lift a bare foot, and whack the roots against the sole of their foot to free them of earth. A spray of silvery water goes flying in the sunlight. The women set the bundles carefully into shallow water to keep the roots wet, then reach down to grasp another handful.

These women are using techniques of cultivating rice by hand that are older than recorded history. The sight of them goes to the psychic core of Angkor and to the practical foundations of its empire.

In the decades after the arrival of the archaeologists, the history of Angkor was gradually unveiled by the epigraphers. One inscription, discovered at Sdok Kak Thom, in the far west of Cambodia, even recorded the moment of birth of the kingdom of Angkor. "His majesty," it reads, "came from Java to reign in the city of Indrapura." The king was Jayavarman II, and he arrived in A.D. 800.

The same year in Rome saw the coronation of Charlemagne, but Jayavarman II was returning to a land in chaos. Only after two years of military campaigns was he strong enough to take the throne.

At the beginning of the ninth century, Cambodia was a vassal state of Java, where the Sailendra dynasty had come to power, claiming to be universal sovereigns. Cambodia was already an old land, known to its own people as Kambuja, after a mythical founder, Kambu; but it was in eclipse, divided by wars of succession.

What little is known of the region's early history is based on the reports of Chinese envoys, who called it Funan. The name comes from the Khmer word *phnom*, meaning "mountain," itself a part of the royal title "king of the mountain." Indian traders and adventurers sailing in on the monsoon winds had already established a religious and architectural legacy. Funan, which extended from the Menam Valley in the west to the Malay peninsula to what is now southern Vietnam, lasted for five hundred years, until the middle of the sixth century, when it was conquered by a vassal kingdom. Called Chenla by the Chinese chroniclers, this was itself eventually subjugated by the Sailendra maharaja.

Why Jayavarman II was in Java is not known. As a young prince, he might have been escaping the dynastic struggles, or he might have been taken prisoner by the Sailendras. His return, however, marked the beginning of the unification of the country. He moved his capital several times, the last three locations being in the region north of the Great Lake, the Tonle Sap. One capital, established within two years of his return, was on the Kulen plateau, about twenty miles north of the lake. Jayavarman then prepared for his coronation, inviting a Brahman priest "to perform a ritual designed to ensure that the country of the Kambujas would no longer be dependent on Java and that there would be no more than one universal monarch." This was, in effect, the Khmer Declaration of Independence. Jayavarman had made himself the new "king of the mountain."

The plateau, however, was far from the fertile land bordering the Tonle Sap and from the lake's rich stock of fish. This drawback was almost certainly a factor in the king's moving the capital yet again, back to an earlier site some ten miles southeast of Angkor. It was in this new capital, Hariharalaya, that Jayavarman spent the rest of his forty-eight-year reign.

Jayavarman not only established the kingdom; he brought with him a concept that dominated Khmer history for centuries and was directly responsible for the way Angkor appears today: the cult of the god-king. Hindu beliefs already formed the basis of worship, but Jayavarman, with the help of the Brahman who had become his priest when he first arrived in the country, made an important change. He identified himself, and all future kings, with a god. In the ninth century, the god was Siva, whose symbol was the *linga*, the stylized phallus, so Jayavarman became the earthly incarnation of Siva. According to the new cult, maintaining this magical association between god and king was critical for guaranteeing the well-being of the realm.

The rituals needed for the cult centered on a sacred image. For Siva, it was naturally a *linga*, and in the new Khmer religion it was called the *kamrateng jagat ta rajya*, "the lord of the universe who is royalty." It was installed in a temple at the center of the kingdom, in a sanctuary tended by the Brahman priests.

The cult had a profound effect on the cities and temples the Khmers built over the following centuries. Each king had his own sacred image containing the royal essence, and for this image a new central temple had to be built. As the Khmer empire grew in size, wealth, and power, the ambitions of its rulers expanded as well, and the temples became ever grander in concept.

Jayavarman II was succeeded by his son, Jayavarman III, who continued his father's work, but it was his successor, Indravarman, who oversaw the construction of the temples that eventually covered more than sixty square miles of the forests and savannas north of the Great Lake. Within a few years of each other, he began three important temples, now known as the Bakong, Preah Ko, and Lolei. Like all the Angkor temples, their modern names are not what they would have been called originally. By the time the Europeans arrived in the nineteenth century, their names were usually derived from legend or from some obvious feature. Lolei contains an echo of the city's name, Hariharalaya. Preah Ko is the Sacred Ox because there were three statues of the Nandin bull, the mount of the god Siva, in front of the row of towers. It was merely a pleasant coincidence that live oxen were grazing at Preah Ko at the time of our visit.

In forging a link between the king and heaven, the temples reaffirmed the religious validity of the new dynasty. In the practical sphere, however, there were natural elements to be conquered: water and rice.

The great Mekong River irrigated Cambodia's broad plains far to the east, ensuring fertile land. And once a year, after the rainy season, the river flows upstream through a tributary to fill the Tonle Sap, the legacy of a prehistoric sea. The region around this Great Lake is one of the easiest places on earth to make a subsistence living. Rice grows with little attention, and as the level of the lake falls each year in the dry season, fish can be hauled out by the basketful. With little more effort, ponds can be dug to trap the water as it recedes.

For more than a subsistence food supply, however, much more effort is needed. The climate is controlled by the monsoon—the seasonal pattern of wind and rain brought on by temperature and atmospheric pressure differences between the Indian Ocean and the Central Asian landmass. Water is a capricious gift: too much and the crops drown, too little and the crops cannot grow. For four months of the year, during Central Asia's summer, Cambodia is deluged by rain, but during the dry season that extends over the rest of the year, the land bakes. The solution, of course, is irrigation. However, storing and distributing water on a large scale becomes an enormous challenge when the available technology offers little more than bricks or blocks of hardened laterite and stone.

The Khmer kings, however, were able to take on this challenge. They were beginning to forge a highly structured society, and with a hierarchy of officials they could organize and undertake large projects. Moreover, they were motivated by their dynastic goal: a succession of great temples which had to be built and supported.

Indravarman understood that a rice surplus was essential and that it was therefore critical to ensure a dependable supply of water. In 877, the first year of his reign, he built a great reservoir just north of the city to retain water through the dry season. Later kings built even larger reservoirs, *barays*. Workers diverted rivers and constructed a network of canals based on a carefully worked out system of water management. Eventually, the fertile plain north of the Tonle Sap was able to yield three, and sometimes four, rice crops a year, providing enough extra food to support each king's artisans and laborers, the ranks of courtiers and slaves, and of course the armies.

In the course of all this building, the capital itself was moved. Indravarman's son succeeded him in 889 and within several years began his own city. First he needed to build a temple to house the sacred *linga*, and he wanted to find a suitably imposing site. The Kulen plateau was too far from rice and water; of the three hills in the area, Phnom Krom was too close to the lake and Phnom Bok was too high and steep. So Phnom Bakheng, the third hill, became the center of the new city of Yasodharapura and the basis of what eventually became known as Angkor, a few miles north of today's Siem Reap. This first city encompassed 6.2 square miles within a moat 656 feet wide. It was crossed by axial avenues and contained about eight hundred artificial ponds. The construction went on for four centuries; eventually the temples spread over an area as large as the island of Manhattan.

The early explorers, like Mouhot, had assumed that the intimate details of the cities would remain hidden forever. Even the inscriptions, which eventually yielded such a wealth of information about the temples, royal history, and administration, say little of everyday life. Fortunately, the bas-reliefs of the Bayon offer timeless glimpses of a society that in some respects survives today in rural Cambodia.

The bas-reliefs show skewered fish on racks, just as we saw near the Tonle Sap. The ancient oxcarts are the same as the contemporary ones, down to the shape of the shafts. The stones show domestic scenes, fishing with nets, bargaining in a market, cockfights and boarfights, cooking, baking clay pots. Some things never change.

Even more informative, however, is the description of ancient Angkor given by a Chinese traveler called Chou Ta-kuan. He spent almost a complete year at Angkor, from 1296 to 1297, assigned to a Mongol embassy. Although he was a diplomat, Chou Ta-kuan wrote more about daily life than affairs of state. Indeed, he seems to have had little access to the palace, possibly because he was Chinese. (As in many Asian countries today, the Chinese, who were traders and businessmen, were not especially loved by the Khmers. The Chinese, in turn, believed themselves innately superior to the southern "barbarians.")

The center of the city's life was the Royal Palace, of which only the foundations remain today. "The tiles of the central dwelling are of lead; other parts of the palace are covered with pottery tiles, yellow in colour. Lintels and columns, all decorated with carved or painted Buddhas, are immense. The roofs, too, are impressive. Long colonnades and open corridors stretch away, interlaced in harmonious relation. . . . I have heard it said that within the palace are many marvellous sights, but these are so strictly guarded that I had no chance to see them.

"Every day the King holds two audiences. No list of agenda is provided. Functionaries and ordinary people who wish to see the Sovereign seat themselves on the ground to await his arrival. In the course of time distant music is heard in the palace, while from outside blasts on conch-shells sound forth as though to welcome the ruler. I have been told that at this point the Sovereign, coming from nearby, contents himself with only one golden palanquin. Two girls of the palace lift up the curtain with their slender fingers and the King, sword in hand, appears standing in the golden window. All present—ministers and commoners—join their hands and touch the earth with their foreheads, lifting up their heads only when the sound of conches has ceased. The Sovereign seats himself at once on a lion's skin, which is an hereditary royal treasure."

In the great square in front of the palace there was such a succession of parades and events that Chou Ta-kuan lost track. For the New Year, fireworks were arranged on tall towers a hundred and twenty feet high. "Rockets and firecrackers are placed on top of these— all this at great expense to the provinces and the noble families," he wrote. "As night comes on, the King is besought to take part in the spectacle. The rockets are fired, and the crackers touched off. The rockets can be seen at a distance of eight miles: the firecrackers, large as swivel-guns, shake the whole city with their explosions." Among the other ceremonies was a census, "when the entire population of the kingdom [was] summoned to the capital and passed in review before the royal palace.

"When the King leaves his palace, the procession is headed by the soldiery; then come the flags, the banners, the music. Girls of the palace, three or five hundred in number, gaily dressed, with flowers in their hair and tapers in their hands, are massed together. . . . Then came still more girls, the bodyguard of the palace, holding shields and lances. . . . Ministers and princes, mounted on elephants, were preceded by bearers of scarlet parasols without number. . . . Finally the Sovereign appeared, standing erect on an elephant and holding in his hand the sacred sword. This elephant, his tusks sheathed in gold, was accompanied by bearers of twenty white parasols with golden shafts." From this Chou Ta-kuan concluded, "It is plain to see that these people, though barbarians, know what is due to a Prince."

Below the king was a whole hierarchy "of ministers, generals, astronomers, and other functionaries; beneath these come all sorts of small employees, differing only in name from our own. . . . The dwellings of the

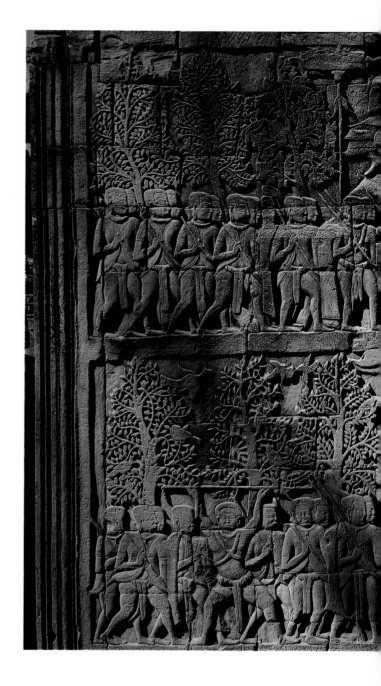

princes and holders of high office are wholly different in size and design from those of the people. The family temple and the main hall are covered with tile; all the outlying buildings are thatched with straw. The rank of every official determines the size of his house.

"Straw thatch covers the dwellings of the commoners, not one of whom would dare place the smallest bit of tile on his roof. In this class, too, wealth determines the size of the house, but no-one would venture to vie with the nobility."

Beginning with the time of Yasodharapura as the capital, the Khmer rulers waged regular wars with their

The Khmer army on the march.

neighbors and extended the borders of the empire. Their chief rival, the only one with an army strong enough to challenge them, was the Chams, in the central coastal part of what is now Vietnam. King Rajendravarman invaded the Cham heartland in about 950 and carried away a golden statue as a trophy. According to the inscriptions, "His brilliance burned the enemy kingdoms, beginning with Champa." In the first half of the eleventh century, the armies of King Suryavarman II pushed west to conquer the Menam Valley, then moved north, attacking states in the Mekong Valley and its tributaries, near what is now the Golden Triangle on the borders of modern Thailand, Burma, and Laos.

Settlement followed conquest. A network of roads connected the distant outposts of the empire, and regional capitals were built. Two of the most important ones were Sukhothai, which eventually became the first capital of the Siamese kingdom, and Phimai, about one hundred and forty miles directly northwest of Angkor across the Dangrek mountain range. The roads made it possible for goods to be traded between countries as far apart as India and China. By the time Suryavarman II came to the throne, the Khmer empire encompassed most of what is now Thailand, the south of Vietnam, Laos, and part of the Malay peninsula. It had surpassed the legendary Funan and become known, even as far away as China, as "Cambodia the rich and noble."

The first major temple to be started close to the Great Lake was the Bakong, on the plain of Roluos where the first king, Jayavarman II, set his capital. It was completed in 881 as the central temple of the city of Hariharalaya, a five-tiered pyramid roughly 200 feet square at the base and about 50 feet high. The central sanctuary at the top was originally built of light materials and has long since disappeared. This tower was replaced by a larger one of sandstone, in ruins when it was discovered by the French. Two conservators were responsible for its reconstruction: Henri Marchal, who collected the debris, and Maurice Glaize, who reassembled it.

Surrounding the pyramid of the Bakong are a number
of towers and annexes, all within a walled enclosure
roughly 380 by 500 feet. Their condition varies; of this
building to the north of the eastern face, only the sandstone frame of the doorway remains. Even at this period, the art of the lintel carving was highly developed.

70

In the corners of the reconstructed tower, bas-relief goddesses stand in arched niches. The pose is stiff and the sculpting rather plain, but such figures set the stage for the development of bas-relief figure carving, which reached its peak with the *apsaras* of Angkor Wat. The dress is typical of the ninth century: naked to the waist with a long skirt, pleated at the front, and jeweled girdles.

The greatest single irrigation work of the empire, the Western Baray, was a reservoir 1.5 miles wide by 8 miles long built by Udayadityavarman II in the middle of the eleventh century. It was constructed not by excavation, but by erecting huge earth dikes that were so effective that, despite silting in the eastern half of the reservoir, it continues to supply irrigation water for the rice fields to the south. A modern sluice gate in its southern dike was built in the 1950s with American aid, making it possible to supply 50 square miles of agricultural land with water.

Under the regime of the monsoons, managing the flow and supply of water was an essential skill, probably even before the Khmer kings organized it on a grand scale. Chou Ta-kuan noted: "In this country it rains half the year; the other half has no rain at all. From the fourth to the ninth moon there is rain every afternoon, and the level of the Great Lake may rise seven to eight fathoms." Cambodian farmers became expert at making the best use of the available supplies. Here on the Siem Reap River, which originally fed a large part of the canal system in and around Angkor, a series of crude but effective waterwheels supply the houses of villagers along its banks.

After water itself, the great resource of the Tonle Sap is fish. Then, as now, the catch was netted from boats. Chou Ta-kuan wrote: "Of all the fish, the black carp is the most abundant; next in number come the ordinary carp, the bastard carp, the tench, and fresh-water congers. There are also gudgeons, which when mature weigh two pounds or more. Other varieties of fish are found, whose names were strange to me. All these fish that I have mentioned come from the Great Lake."

Competing for the haul of fish is a crocodile, a species that used to be more abundant. The diplomat continued: "Crocodiles there are, large as boats, which have four feet and are exactly like dragons, with no horns however. Their belly is delicious to eat."

73

Rice has always been the staple of the region, and the methods of cultivation have changed little. The irrigation projects of the Khmer kings supplemented the seasonal inundation of the rice fields. Chou Ta-kuan wrote: "Generally speaking, three or four crops a year can be counted on, for the entire Cambodian year resembles the fifth and sixth moons of China, and frost and snow are unknown." "Farmers who have noted when the rice is ripe and the height to which the water then rises in flood, time their sowing according to these findings." "There is, moreover, a certain kind of land where the rice grows naturally, without sowing. When the water is up one fathom, the rice keeps pace in its growth. This, I think, must be a special variety."

The rice was kept in covered woven baskets, and it was usually eaten by hand, without a utensil. Both these scenes from daily life are from the bas-reliefs on the outer gallery of the Bayon. Chou Ta-kuan observed that "only their fingers are used in eating rice, which is sticky." The rice must have been the glutinous variety eaten today throughout the Laotian-speaking parts of the region, to the north; the grains adhere to each other and are easiest to eat in this manner.

(preceding page)

One of the earliest temples built after the capital was
moved from Roluos to Angkor at the end of the ninth
century was Prasat Kravan (its modern name, meaning
Cardamom Sanctuary). Although completed in A.D.
921, it was unusual in that it was built of brick, a common material before the establishment of the Khmer
kingdom but already, by the tenth century, superseded
by laterite and sandstone. In the northernmost tower,
open at the top, bas-reliefs depict Vishnu's consort,
Lakshmi, and her attendants.

Three decades after Prasat Kravan and about 3 miles to the northeast, the temple of East Mebon was completed in A.D. 952 in the middle of the great East Baray, which was only a little smaller than the later West Baray. In the course of building the reservoir, the Siem Reap River was diverted to run around its north and west sides. Chou Ta-kuan later wrote: "The Eastern Lake lies some two and a half miles east of the Walled City. . . . At its centre stands a stone tower, with dozens of stone chambers." There is a puzzle in this de-scription, because he went on to describe "a recumbent bronze Buddha, from whose navel flows a steady stream of water." A statue fitting this description was indeed discovered, in 1936, but in the middle of the West Baray. Chou Ta-kuan's accuracy in the remainder of his account makes it strange that he confused the two.

Rising from the center of what was once the Royal Palace, the pyramid temple of the Phimeanakas was probably built around A.D. 970. Its name derives from two Sanskrit words, *vimana* and *akasa*, which together mean Celestial, or Flying, Palace. Although smaller than the majority of Angkor's temples, it was still sufficiently important at the time of Chou Ta-kuan's visit for the emissary to recount a curious rite that was supposed to take place on its summit, to ensure the prosperity of the kingdom. He wrote: "Out of the palace rises a golden tower, to the top of which the ruler ascends nightly to sleep. It is common belief that in the tower dwells a genie, formed like a serpent with nine heads, which is Lord of the entire kingdom. Every night this genie appears in the shape of a woman, with whom the sovereign couples. . . . Should the genie fail to appear for a single night, it is a sign that the King's death is at hand. If, on the other hand, the King should fail to keep his tryst, disaster is sure to follow." Lions guard the steep staircase that leads to the upper terrace.

The towers of Pre Rup stand on an upper terrace covering a little more than 300 square feet and set almost 50 feet above the surrounding countryside. The brick towers were originally decorated elaborately with plaster, but most of it has now fallen off. The doorways are of particular interest, with fine lintels and colonnettes. Pre Rup is near the eastern extremity of the Angkor temples and close to the southern dike of the East Baray, an enormous reservoir that has now dried up.

The temple of Takeo, completed a few decades after Pre Rup, was the first to be built entirely in sandstone. On the upper terrace, almost 40 feet high and reached by steep staircases, stand five towers. The central tower, at the right in the photograph, is on a base almost 20 feet high; the others are on 3-foot bases. The large blocks used in this new departure in Khmer architecture must have been difficult to dress and assemble, and construction was halted when only a few of them were carved. The plain finish of the masonry contributes to its massive feeling.

Although the exact date is not known, the Baphuon was the next major temple to be built, in the middle of the eleventh century. Close to the center of the walled city of Angkor Thom and a short walk north and west of the Bayon, it was an imposing temple in its time. The central pyramid, now in a state of ruin, had a base of about 300 by 400 feet set within an enclosure of about 400 by 1,400 feet. The eastern pavilion on the lower level of the pyramid (above) is today the best preserved part. In this relatively early period of con-struction at Angkor, the narrative bas-reliefs were carved in the form of panels. The inspiration for most of them was the Hindu epic tradition, in particular the legends of Rama and Krishna, both incarnations of the god Vishnu. Within each panel, only two or three fig-ures are usually shown, along with some simple ele-ments to convey the setting. Bernard-Philippe Groslier, the last French conservator, thought that the sculptors were imitating the effect of a shadow-puppet theater, the popular way of presenting these epics.

Consecrated to Siva and just outside the later walls of the city of Angkor Thom, Chaosay Tevoda is one of two neighboring temples that architecturally appear to come just before Angkor Wat. At the left of the photograph, false windows line the eastern end of the hall that extends from the sanctuary; they are surrounded by decorations of roseate panels and female divinities. The hall faces onto the east entrance pavilion, the best preserved, with three linked passages and an upper story. A short causeway on pillars links the hall and pavilion.

Opposite Chaosay Tevoda on the road leading east
from the Victory Gate, the temple of Thommanon has
a similar layout of a central sanctuary with a tower, a
main entrance facing east, and three blind entrances.
Nothing remains of the enclosure except the two entrance pavilions; the western one shown here now stands
alone. Beyond it, the central tower has the cone shape
with projecting acrotera reminiscent of the towers of
Angkor Wat.

The king in his court, carved in bas-relief at the beginning of the thirteenth century on what is now known as the Terrace of the Leper King (named after a famous statue found above it). Next to him, a female member of the court reaches for a betel box; nearby, a sword swallower performs his entertainment. When Chou Ta-kuan attended the court at the end of the century, he wrote of the king: "On his head he carries a diadem much like those worn by the vajradhara. . . . Round his neck he wears some three pounds of great pearls. On wrists, ankles and fingers he wears bracelets and rings of gold, all set with cat's eyes. His feet are bare. The soles of his feet and the palms of his hands are stained with henna. On leaving the palace he wears a golden sword."

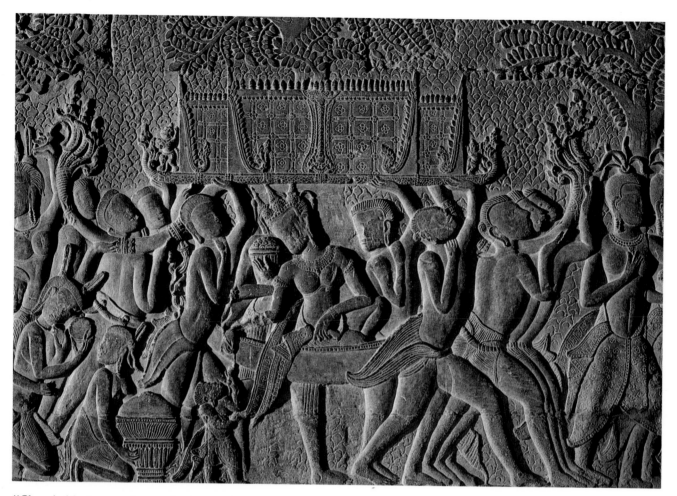

"Close behind come the royal wives and concubines, in palanquins and chariots," wrote Chou Ta-kuan. On a bas-relief at Angkor Wat, one of five queens rides in a great procession, with bearers and attendants. "Palanquins are made from one piece of wood, curved in the middle," he continued, "with the two ends rising vertically, and carved with flowery motifs plated with gold or silver. At the distance of one foot from each end a hook is fastened and to these hooks a large piece of material, folded loosely, is attached with cords. The passenger sinks into this litter and two men bear him away. . . . The highest dignitaries use palanquins with golden shafts and two-handled parasols."

Female court attendants mount steps, one carrying a parasol, the other a container for betel nuts. The Chinese traveler wrote: "Generally speaking, the women, like the men, wear only a strip of cloth, bound round the waist, showing bare breasts of milky whiteness. Their hair is fastened up in a knot, and they go barefoot, even the wives of the King, who are five in number." A kettle can be seen under the stairs.

Wild animals abounded in the Angkor period of Cambodia's history. Dynamically carved on the Bayon's eastern outer gallery, hunters have captured a wild buffalo. According to Chou Ta-kuan, "Wild buffaloes, by hundreds and by thousands, graze in groups in this region." There are three species, and although this carved animal was identified by Commaille as a *khting*, the Khmer word for "gaur," the shape of the horns suggests a more interesting possibility, the kouprey. This extremely rare animal was first described scientifically in 1937, the year that the first live specimen was sent to the Paris zoo. In 1969, just before civil war reached the area, it was estimated that there were only one hundred left. The most obvious field characteristic of a bull kouprey is that the curve of the horns starts convex from the base, dipping down and then upward and forward (the other species' horns have a simple concave curve).

The importance of elephants is stressed by their frequent appearance in the architecture—as corner guardians on the terraces of temples such as Pre Rup, as motifs at the base of the gate towers of the city of Angkor Thom, and particularly bordering the main square of the city. Here, along a great terrace, almost 50 feet wide and 1,200 feet long, a line of elephants in relief is depicted hunting. The Terrace of the Elephants was originally the basement of a hall that was part of the palace complex.

(preceding page)

"Soldiers also move about unclothed and barefoot. In the right hand is carried a lance, in the left a shield. They have no bows, no arrows, no slings, no missiles, no breastplates, no helmets." This description from Chou Ta-kuan at the end of the thirteenth century could have been made at almost any point in Khmer history. Despite the simplicity of arms and lack of protection, the campaign successes that gave Angkor's kings control over the bulk of the Southeast Asian mainland demonstrate the ability of the army.

Throughout Khmer history there were periods of expansion, much of it aggressive. The two great themes of Khmer bas-reliefs are scenes from Hindu mythology and celebrations of the might of the king and his army. On the east face of the Bayon's outer gallery, soldiers rush into battle over the bodies of the fallen; in another detail, slaves are roped together around their necks.

(opposite)

The country's principal enemy throughout the Angkor period was the neighboring kingdom of Champa, in what is now central Vietnam. Also an Indianized state, Champa was in a more precarious situation, for it was regularly threatened by China, to the north. In the battle scenes of the Bayon's bas-reliefs, the Chams are depicted with a distinctive headdress in the form of an inverted lotus flower and with a more Chinese cast to the face than the Khmers.

(preceding page)

Although the exact relationship between Angkor and the Khmer settlements of the Korat plateau, to the north, is still in doubt, this part of what is now Thailand was the subject of early Khmer campaigns. One of the most prominent temples, now meticulously restored, is Phnom Rung. Standing on an extinct volcano (its name means "large hill") some 20 miles north of the range that forms the modern border of Cambodia and Thailand, it was subject to a number of additions and rebuilding. The distinctive lotus-shaped tower was built during the reign of Suryavarman II, at about the same time as Angkor Wat, although there is evidence of earlier construction from the tenth century. In the foreground is part of a laterite hall.

(opposite)

The quality of the carving of this northern temple is considered by some to be the finest of the Angkor period. Lunet de Lajonquière, who made an inventory of the Khmer ruins and, in 1907, first described Phnom Rung in detail, wrote that "in plan, execution and decoration it is among the most perfect of its kind." Over the west entrance to the sanctuary, an elaborate *fronton* represents a famous scene from the *Ramayana;* the form of Phnom Rung's tower is worked into it. The flying palace, escorted by monkeys and supported by a row of *hamsa* (the sacred geese), is the *pushpaka.* In it reclines Sita, who has been sent by the demon Ravana to witness the death of her husband, Rama. The extraordinary amount of detail packed into the limited space without any sense of overcrowding is typical of this period of Khmer stonework.

The main entrance to the temple is the pavilion facing east; through the doorway can be seen the alignment of entrances all the way through the hall and sanctuary. On the pediment is the image of Siva as an ascetic—in effect, the first image presented to anyone entering the temple. The inscriptions suggest that it is also the image of a yogi-warrior called Narendratitya, a contemporary of Suryavarman II, in whose army he may have been a commander. He is described in inscriptions as "a very important guru who is one and the same with Siva of the large hill" and "meditating in a dark cave he diffused a light more brilliant than the sun itself."

The tower of Phnom Rung is seen through the south
doorway of the gallery that surrounds the courtyard.
The temple faces south toward Angkor, and studies of
the iconography show that the carvings on this side of
the sanctuary tower and hall had a special importance.

Only 3 miles from Phnom Rung, at the foot of the hill, is the older temple of Muang Tam, dating from the latter part of the tenth century and completed by Jayavarman V. A laterite wall encloses a rectangular area that contains four symmetrically sited pools. At first glance, these pools have the appearance of a broad moat that surrounds the inner courtyard. Subsidence has affected this temple, as can be seen above in the northeast pool and the collapsed north entrance pavilion. A *baray* north of the temple still contains water.

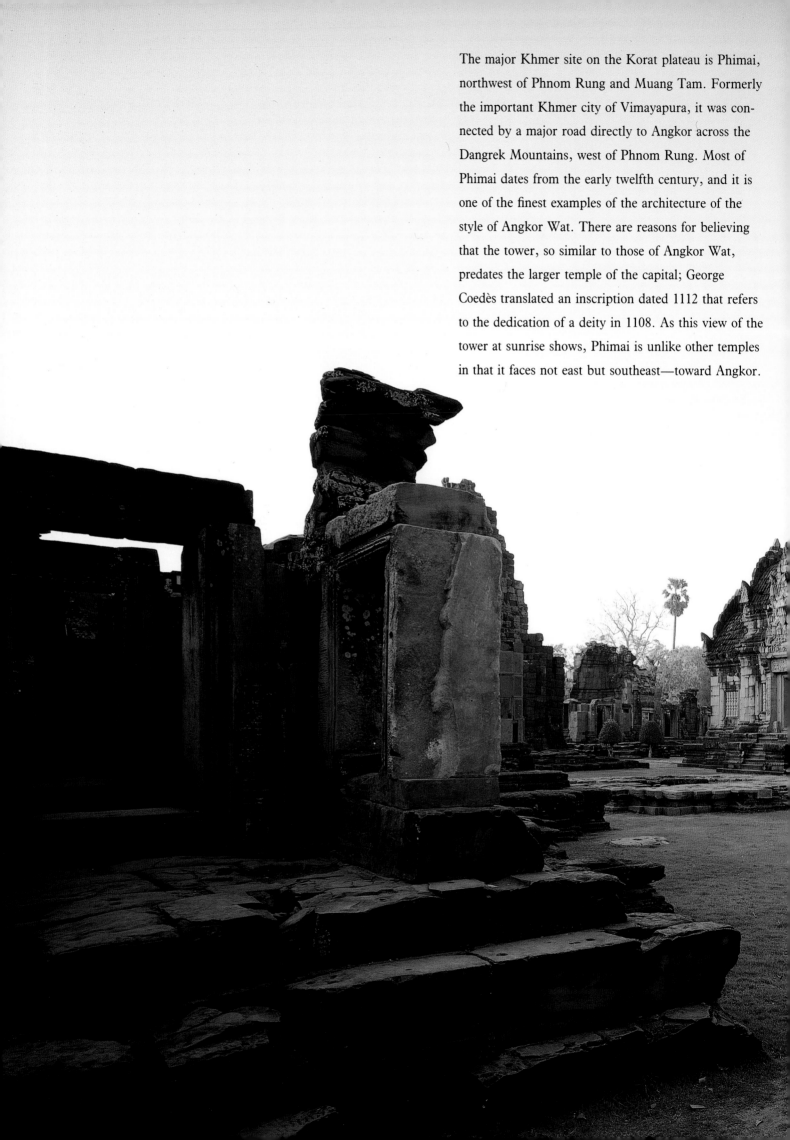

The major Khmer site on the Korat plateau is Phimai, northwest of Phnom Rung and Muang Tam. Formerly the important Khmer city of Vimayapura, it was connected by a major road directly to Angkor across the Dangrek Mountains, west of Phnom Rung. Most of Phimai dates from the early twelfth century, and it is one of the finest examples of the architecture of the style of Angkor Wat. There are reasons for believing that the tower, so similar to those of Angkor Wat, predates the larger temple of the capital; George Coedès translated an inscription dated 1112 that refers to the dedication of a deity in 1108. As this view of the tower at sunrise shows, Phimai is unlike other temples in that it faces not east but southeast—toward Angkor.

Close to Phimai, one of the smaller temples on the plateau is Phnom Wan, built mainly in the early tenth century during the reign of Suryavarman I. The central sanctuary was surrounded by a rectangular laterite wall and moat; it consists of a rectangular sanctuary tower extending to an antechamber. False and open balustered windows line the sides, and a fine lintel is visible here over the north doorway to the main sanctuary.

Discovered in 1939 in the temple of Preah Khan and still standing there, this important stele glorifies the temple's builder, King Jayavarman VII, his family, and "the religion of Sakyamuni," Buddhism of the Greater Vehicle. More prosaically, it gives a detailed inventory for the provisioning of Preah Khan, which was dedicated in 1191. This and many other stone inscriptions are the source of most of our detailed knowledge of Khmer history. It was translated from the Sanskrit by George Coedès, the doyen of French scholars.

"The sun in this heaven that is the family of Sri Kambu, born on this rising mountain that is Jayadityapura, this splendid treasure, supreme king of Sresthapura, awoke the hearts of living beings like the lotus."

"Seeing the terrible appearance in combat of this king equipped with his weapons, the enemies closed their eyes and their arms, like serpents, let their arrows fall, while the spears that they had long before thrown seemed to be halted in mid-air."

"The King and the owners of villages have devoutly given 5,324 villages,
totalling 97,840 men and women,
444 chefs;
4,606 footmen, cooks and others;
2,298 servants, of which 1,000 dancers;
47,436 individuals making sacrificial offerings."

"I honour the supreme path which leads to higher enlightenment, the unique doctrine which offers no obstacle to attaining understanding of reality, the Law which the Immortals of the three worlds must honour, the sword which destroys the jungle of the six inner passions (desire, anger, greed, distraction, pride, and envy)."

"Here is what should be in the royal storehouses each year:

Rice: 1,328 khari, 2 drona;

Gold objects: 253 towers and other objects. 18,160 hemispherical dishes and other utensils.

Peas: 57 khari, 3 drona;
Sesame: 29 kharika, 3 drona, 4 prastha;

112,300 pearls;
Bronze: 16,110 bhara, 3 tula, 1 katti, 10 pana."

The Magic Mountain

On the crest of this mountain of gold, in a temple of gold, shining with celestial brilliance, he erected a *linga* of Siva, honored with ablutions at the prescribed times.

—From the stele at Lovek

We have spent the cool morning hours in the Bayon. Inside, it's an astonishing puzzle-palace of terraces and stairways, bas-relief sculptures and huge stone faces taller than the height of a man. From a distance, though, it simply looks like a jumbled pyramid, a heap of stones covered with lichen.

By noon our shirts are soaked with perspiration, and we drink from our canteens. At the horizon, the sky is a hazy, milky white. From straight overhead, the sun beats down. Its fierce ultraviolet rays have leached the colors from the landscape. The colors will only freshen toward late afternoon unless we are lucky enough to get a rainstorm, which isn't likely.

But if the colors are flat, the landscape isn't. Looking away from the Bayon, we glimpse a drab green mound through the trees to the northwest. In the harsh light of noon, it looks very big. Consulting our maps, we find that it's an unrestored manmade mountain, the Baphuon.

We decide to hike there and climb it. The stone steps are very steep and covered by dirt and grass. Below we see a concrete slab, left two decades ago by the French when the civil war got worse. Nearby lies a rusty construction crane, wrecked by Pol Pot's Khmer Rouge. Finally, we reach the top.

Below in the distance we see figures walking leisurely along the road. Buddhist monks in orange robes carry black umbrellas as protection against the sun. The monks are a recurring grace note at Angkor. They often stroll through the ruins, calm and serene. The sight of them is always refreshing.

The monks belong to the Theravada branch of Buddhism, which is practiced in Cambodia, Sri Lanka, Burma, Thailand, and Laos. The monks we see from the top of the Baphuon live in the modern *wat* (temple) nearby. Two more Buddhist monasteries flank Angkor Wat itself, between the main building and the outer enclosure; other monasteries and shrines containing Buddhist statues are scattered throughout the Angkor region.

For several centuries, Cambodians have traveled great distances to worship at Angkor. When Henri Mouhot and the other early explorers arrived, they noted that Angkor Wat was a destination for Buddhist pilgrims. It was natural for them to assume that the temples had been Buddhist from the start; even the great hooded cobras that form the parapets of the causeway had a place in Buddhist mythology.

But the Westerners arriving a few decades later, the scholars of the École Française d'Extrême-Orient, knew better. Many of the bas-reliefs, they pointed out, showed scenes from the great Hindu epics. One was the *Mahabharata, The Great Epic of the Bharata Dynasty,* written sometime between 400 B.C. and A.D. 200; it recounts the feud between two Indian dynasties. Another, with an even more distinctive cast of characters, was the *Ramayana,* an epic romance of Hindu deities, heroes, and demons that became a popular morality tale.

Hindu mythology dates from about 1400 B.C., when the earliest known religious texts were written. They were the first of the Vedas, the Books of Knowledge, and they celebrated the principal gods of India. There was a great pantheon of Hindu gods whose importance in relation to one another changed over the centuries. Some of the earliest gods faded from the spectrum of worship while others, who appeared first as mere helpers, rose to prominence. The Vedic texts themselves span a thousand years from first to last. By the time the final verses were written, during the classical period of Hindu mythologizing, only three major gods remained: Brahma, Vishnu, and Siva, who made up the Trimurti, the Hindu trinity.

A philosophy had begun to emerge, a cosmology in which the gods played roles symbolizing the forces of existence. Their arena was the universe itself and the issues were elemental: the creation and destruction of all things and the struggle between order and chaos.

In Hinduism, Brahma is the ultimate creator, the four-headed god who can oversee the whole of existence. Strangely, though, he was worshiped only occasionally, and a great Brahma cult never developed. Worship was focused on either Vishnu or Siva, who between them represent the underlying, essential conflict of existence. Vishnu is the preserver, the god of order, and tries to maintain harmony. In times of danger he can take on an earthly form—as a superhuman being or as an animal endowed with magic—and battle with the agents threatening human existence. Almost a godly white knight, Vishnu acts for the good of mankind and so easily inspires devotion.

The dark side of existence is represented by Siva, the destroyer, who embodies all the remote and terrible aspects of heaven. Siva is the ultimate agent of chaos who, at the end of each eon, dances the universe to its destruction. If Vishnu inspires devotion, Siva is unpredictable and has to be propitiated. He destroys by violent action and also sows destruction by decay, through the agency of time. From total destruction grows the seed of life, however, so that when Siva brings the universe to an end, he is preparing the way for its rebirth—a concept embodied in modern physics.

Whether the Hindu priests arrived by chance or the Khmer rulers sought them is not known, but Cambodia's religious conversion was peaceful. The two godly antagonists, Vishnu and Siva, attracted worshipers in turn, and at different times one or the other was the favorite Khmer god. At Angkor, the ninth and tenth centuries were devoted to the worship of Siva, but the pendulum then swung toward Vishnu, the god celebrated in the culmination of Khmer architecture, Angkor Wat. Even so, there was a considerable tolerance of worship between the two. In some temples, the images of Vishnu and Siva exist side by side, and at one period before the settling of Angkor, the two appeared as a god with a split personality, Harihara: the left side of his body was Vishnu, the right side Siva. Hariharalaya, the city designed by the first Khmer king, was named after this god.

The rulers' obsession with building temples continued until the early thirteenth century, ending with a burst of construction under the last of the great kings, Jayavarman VII. The fact that each king needed his own temple in order to house his sacred *linga* does not explain the scale and virtuosity of the architecture. Certainly, once it was realized that these were temples to Hindu gods, the references to the cosmology in the carvings were obvious. In one gallery of Angkor Wat a bas-relief depicts the creation myth, elsewhere the exploits of Vishnu, and in another pavilion Siva. But the effect of Hindu cosmology went much further, and the temples had another, essential function that was not at all obvious to Western eyes.

Underpinning the religious ideas brought from India was a fundamental view of the world in which there was a magical relationship between earth and heaven, between the world of human beings and the entire universe. Whatever happened on earth, from the trivial to the significant, every event, every creature, was controlled by cosmic forces, and it was essential that everything in the kingdom was kept in harmony with these forces. All the religious practices, including the cult of the relationship between god and king, were performed to this harmonious end. And because the magical relationship between the earth and the universe went both ways, the Khmers devised the idea of building replicas of the universe on earth.

The temples of Angkor, the scholars of the École realized, were meant to be microcosms of the universe. With this single insight, the structure of the temples, their decorations, their plans—all became clear. At the center of the world in Hindu cosmology is a continent, Jambudvipa. Encircling it are six rings of mountain ranges, the Cakravala, and seven oceans. The outermost ocean is enclosed by a gigantic wall of rock. At the center of the central continent rises Mount Meru, the cosmic mountain, the axis of the universe. On its summit, with its five peaks, is the home of the gods.

This concept of building an earthly replica of a region of the heavens was not invented by the Khmers. It was part of the inherited tradition from India, where the Sanskrit word *pratibimba* encompasses the idea of representing the cosmos with a model. Yet nowhere else was it followed to such perfection as at Angkor. In India itself, there are no pyramid temples with five towers to represent Mount Meru's summit.

The representation in Angkor was purely symbolic. It was never thought necessary to build an exact model of the continent, the mountain, and the six rings of seas and mountain ranges. Instead, these essential features were translated into architecture, and its evolution took time. Engineering techniques had to be developed, and the succession of monuments shows that in dealing with structural problems, the Khmers were feeling their way. Their first material, brick, was too limiting to produce anything on a massive scale. For this reason, some of the early temple-mountains used natural peaks for the basic shape. Building mountains on flat ground was a different matter, calling for enormous quantities of material: laterite blocks in the early attempts, then sandstone as the skill and confidence of the builders grew.

The most essential element in reproducing the cosmos was the mountain, Meru, the home of the gods. The solution was the pyramid, in itself not original to the Khmers. The Mesopotamians and Egyptians had used pyramids long before. The Bakong, center of the original Khmer city by the Great Lake, was the first Cambodian temple-mountain in the form of a pyramid. Built in A.D. 881, it was followed by the Bakheng and others, such as the Phimeanakas, in the center of the Royal Palace.

116

What distinguishes the Khmer pyramids from others in the ancient world is their degree of symbolism, not only in the principal structure but also in the outbuildings, which are part of an elaborate and talismanic whole. A simple pyramid was not enough. The kings and their architects wanted to guarantee a magical effect and set about reproducing the other elements of the universe and refining the detail. Mount Meru, for example, was supposed to have five peaks. The Khmers devised a literal version: a quincunx of towers on the summit of the pyramid. One tower was in the middle, typically higher or larger than the four others that surrounded it at the corners of a square. These towers were built on the Bakheng, in the center of the first capital on the Angkor site, followed by the temple of the East Mebon. The Bakheng had the advantage of a natural hill, but the East Mebon was built on the plain, and its builders did not attempt a high pyramid to support the towers. A few years later, however, they successfully erected the first true temple-mountain, called Pre Rup, built up from level ground and with a quincunx of towers. Another innovation followed with the construction of Takeo, the first temple-mountain made entirely from sandstone.

The representation of the concentric seas and ranges around Meru presented a further challenge. The answer was at first very simple. A single wall would represent the mountains; a single moat, the sea. For the Khmers, of course, water had a practical as well as a cosmological significance. They used water to grow rice, their staple food. The elaborate system of *barays* (reservoirs) and irrigation channels built by the succession of kings was the foundation of Angkor's prosperity. Little wonder, then, that the life-giving water system was held in religious awe.

Maintaining this prosperity was one of the most vital functions of the Khmer religion. The ceremonies performed by the powerful priestly caste were designed to reaffirm the link between the king and heaven. As an earthly manifestation of a god, the king interceded on behalf of his realm to ensure that the waters of heaven would continue to flow. The importance of water ran through several levels of Khmer civilization, from the need to supply and increase the rice crop to the requirements of the temples for ritual use.

The distinction between water for the economy and water for religious symbolism blurred, as did the distinctions between the secular and spiritual in the life of

Angkor. Irrigation channels and temple moats had the same source; the diversion of the Siem Reap River, for instance, had two purposes. Temples were built at the centers of the great *barays* to benefit from the symbolism of a surrounding sea.

Still, the Khmers strove for greater elaboration; and as they did, their architecture emerged as unique. No other ancient civilization attempted such perfect symbolism. The concentric rings of sea and continent became reflected in concentric enclosures in the architecture. Galleries nested within each other and surrounded by an outer wall, all enclosing the central sanctuary, became a feature of Angkor's temples.

The decoration, too, became distinctive. In Hindu cosmology, a rainbow is the bridge to heaven, and the rainbow is linked to the image of a water serpent, the mythical *naga*. This serpent, though known throughout South and Southeast Asia, was used so much at Angkor and other temple sites that it became identified with Khmer architecture. A serpent-arch crowned the lintels over temple entrances during some periods, a symbol of crossing from earth to heaven. *Naga* balustrades line stairways, causeways, and bridges across moats, all heightening the symbolism of the bridge between the worlds. When Buddhism came to Angkor generations later, the *nagas* were accepted without qualm, even though in Buddhist iconography serpents mean something quite different—the wise cobra that spread its hood protectively over the meditating Lord Buddha, when Buddha was trying to reach enlightenment. But then, Indian religions tend to be syncretic. Differing beliefs are accepted as overlapping truths, thereby avoiding much argument between devotees.

Perhaps even more symbolism waits to be uncovered. For example, numbers are known to play a part even beyond the five towers of Meru's summit. There have been interpretations of the dimensions of the temples and the numbers of steps and other elements that suggest the deliberate use of magical numbers. Eleanor Mannika, an American art historian, has suggested the significance of certain distances within Angkor Wat when measured in Khmer units of length: both the distance across the moat's bridge and that from the bridge to the sanctuary correspond to eras in Hindu mythology.

Nothing could have been more different from the architectural developments in the West at the same time. The Gothic period was flowering in Europe, with spacious naves to hold large congregations. At Angkor, the temples were for worship, but the worship of an elite. The important rituals were conducted exclusively by the royal priest, and the style of the sanctuaries reflects this. The architectural oddity of primitive vaulting was in fact no disadvantage: large numbers of worshipers were not wanted, and there was no need to build great halls. For while the cathedrals of Europe were soaring structures celebrating the glory of God, the Khmer architects were attempting something more literal and in a sense more ambitious: they were building a home for the gods on earth.

The temples were talismans on a massive scale. In the macrocosm—the universe—Mount Meru extends into the lower reaches of heaven and equally far below to the underworld. It is the axis of the universe. The Khmers strove to reproduce even it, to the extent of constructing the bases of some temples so that they could not be seen. This was discovered only during excavations by the École, at the Baphuon, and at the Terrace of the Leper King a few hundred yards to the northeast. Carved walls were built and then built over by a second carved layer that completely hid them. The decoration, too, was produced not for the eyes of men but for the pleasure of the gods. Nothing shows this more clearly than the location of the carvings. They are not just on the facades but in corners and angles where few people would think of looking, some even in gaps too narrow to squeeze into. By the end of the eleventh century, the mix of elements needed to create this microcosm was becoming coherent. The king who built the Baphuon, Udayadityavarman II, "thought it fitting to have a Meru in the centre of his capital" and lavished every possible refinement on it. He surrounded his temple-mountain with concentric enclosures, pavilions, and other buildings, met by a long axial causeway. Our predecessor, the observant Chou Ta-kuan, saw the Baphuon still in its prime, its summit covered in bronze, "a truly astonishing spectacle."

The bronze was long gone by the time we climbed to the top of the Baphuon one hot day toward the close of the twentieth century, and so were many of the outbuildings, blurring the coherence of the original layout. But we knew we were on a temple-mountain. With the building of the Baphuon in about A.D. 1060, the stage was set for the building, a century later, of the crowning achievement of Khmer architecture and the most perfect representation of Meru: Angkor Wat.

Vishnu, the less fearful of the two principal Hindu gods worshiped by the Khmers, is usually represented with a cylindrical miter on his head and four arms. When still intact, the arms hold a conch, a disk, a sphere or lotus representing the earth, and a club or sword. The temple of Angkor Wat was dedicated to Vishnu, and although it later became a shrine for Theravada Buddhists, this large statue of Vishnu in galleries of the western entrance is still worshiped.

(opposite)

Of all the religious icons, the most sacred over the longest period of Khmer history was the *linga*. This stylized phallus, of Hindu origin, was the image of Siva—more properly, of the essence of the god. Embedded in a pedestal shaped to allow the drainage of lustral water poured over it, the *linga* typically has a succession of cross sections: from square at the base through octagonal to round. These symbolize, in order, the trinity of Brahma, Vishnu, and Siva. The small sanctuary was intended for priestly ritual, not public worship. On the walls are carvings of Vishnu in various forms: Khmer worship frequently tolerated a combination of the gods.

Water was central to Khmer religious life and cosmology. The Brahman priests anointed the holy image of the god-king with lustral water, the moats surrounding the temples were earthly representations of the ocean surrounding the world, and the artificial lake of Srah Srang was probably used for ritual bathing. Steps leading down to the water face the sunrise and are flanked with lions and the ubiquitous water serpent, the *naga*.

A Sanskrit inscription compares the reservoirs of Angkor with the Ganges and its tributary in India, where they meet at the site of Prayaga, the ancient city where Allahabad now stands: "Prayaga should be approached with the respect worthy of its proximity to the two holy waters. What can we then say of the city of Jayasri, made illustrious by the holy waters consecrated to the Buddha, Siva and Vishnu?"

Water was essential for sacred use, from anointing images to ritual bathing. An inscription on the stele of Preah Khan even notes that neighboring countries paid homage by sending holy water: "The brahmans, beginning with Sri Syryabhatta, the king of Java, the king of the Yavana and the two kings of the Chams, bring water with reverence each day." On a smaller scale than Srah Srang, individual temples were supplied with water for religious rites; it was often kept in basins constructed for the purpose. Although all of these basins have long since dried up, those at the entrance to Phnom Rung, 100 miles north of Angkor, have been restored.

122

Inextricably linked to water were the *nagas*, the many-headed serpents that play an important part in the Hindu mythology that the Khmers drew on for their architectural inspiration. There was even a Cambodian legend that told the story of how the son of an Indian king had seized power here, marrying the *naga* daughter of the serpent king who had helped him conquer the country. The *naga* legends certainly go back to India, but snake cults may have had even earlier origins. At Angkor, the stone balustrade was an innovative way of representing the *naga;* at the end, the serpent rears up with its many-headed hood extended.

Nagas also appeared on sanctuary towers, particularly
those in the style of Angkor Wat, which were characterized by large numbers of acroters, corner projections
that contributed to the intricate outline of the tower.

126

Nagas feature at the bases of the arches that frame the typical Khmer *fronton* above entrances. This feature has been copied in the construction of Theravada Buddhist temples in the region.

This statue of Buddha seated on the coils of a *naga* illustrates a well-known episode from the life of Buddha. A storm raged and torrential rain poured for a whole week. The king of the *nagas,* Muchilinda, came up from the earth to shelter Buddha as he meditated, coiling its body to form a seat and swelling its great hood as protection from the rain. It is Style of the Bayon, late twelfth to early thirteenth century.

Temple decoration served a purpose. Above all, prominent surfaces such as the *fronton,* or pediment, were used to illustrate scenes from Hindu mythology. This *fronton* from Banteay Srei, carved in the third quarter of the ninth century some 20 miles north of Angkor, shows the battle between Bhima and Duryodh.

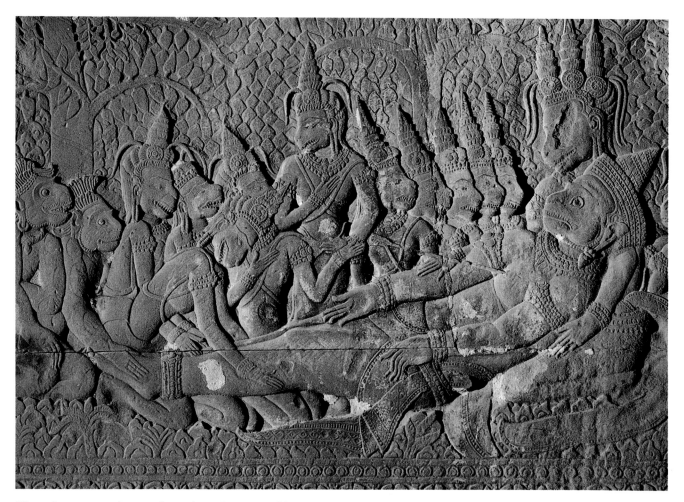

The other extremely popular epic and source of inspiration for the bas-relief carvers was the *Ramayana*, the romantic odyssey of the god Vishnu in one of his earthly forms. Early in the saga, Rama becomes involved in the bitter dispute between the king of the monkeys, Bali, and his brother Surgriva. Rama has promised to help Surgriva in the forthcoming fight and shoots his arrow at Bali. "And a mighty shaft, like unto a thunderbolt and resembling flaming fire, being hurled by Rama, alighted on the breast of Bali. Being wounded by that shaft, that highly powerful chief of monkeys, gifted with prowess, fell down on the earth." Dying, he repents for having usurped the throne. "Bali, ranging on the verge of death, casting his looks around and sighing faintly, espied his younger brother

Surgriva before him. Welcoming that lord of monkeys with clear accents, Bali addressed him affectionately, saying, 'O Surgriva, do thou not take to thy heart the improper conduct I have shown towards thee, being attracted by inevitable foolishness, subject as I was to sin.' To his son he says, 'Do thou not cultivate too much of friendship nor be wanting in it—for both of these extremes are sources of disasters. Do thou therefore follow the golden mean.' After he had said this, his eyes became expanded, his teeth were opened and his appearance became ghastly. And greatly pained by the shaft he breathed his last. And thereupon, the monkeys, the foremost of those who go jumping, having lost their chief, bewailed and cried."

After Rama himself, the best-loved character in the *Ramayana* is Hanuman, the monkey-general. Rama meets Hanuman as he travels in search of his wife, Sita, who has been kidnapped by the demon Ravana. Rama needs to find soldiers for the battle with Ravana, and Hanuman offers to help. He is more than a monkey, however; he is also a god, which Rama notices immediately. "When he looked at the monkey, he recognized the signs of a god: this monkey had a diamond coronet, flashing earrings, and jeweled teeth like no forest ape." When Hanuman's uncle Surgriva becomes king of the monkeys on the death of his brother Bali, the monkey kingdom sides with Rama. In the entire epic, Hanuman is the character with the most personality: he is volatile, brave, a loyal friend, irresistibly attracted to women, and a joker.

Entrances are capped by elaborate *frontons*. Their chief element is an undulating arch that has survived, little changed in style, in modern Buddhist temples in Cambodia, Thailand, and Laos. It derives ultimately from the Indian horseshoe arch and, among other purposes, conceals the ugly finish of the projecting stone blocks used in the corbeled vault behind. The Khmers elaborated the basic form of the arch and incorporated yet another mythological creature, the *makara*. Two of these sea monsters, which were already a part of Indianized architecture in Java, framed each side of the arch with their bodies. Further decoration surrounded the frame of the arch in the form of leaping flames.

The head of a *makara*, typically with a scaly body and the claws of a bird of prey—and in some representations with an elephantine trunk—appears at the base of the arch, one on each side. As a denizen of the sea, it had a natural connection with the *nagas*, and in the *makara* arch, the many-headed serpent emerges from its mouth.

It was in the lintels that the stone carvers excelled. Henri Parmentier, who had trained as an architect and was the chief of the archaeological service of the École Française d'Extrême-Orient until the beginning of the 1930s, considered the lintel "the major decorative point of the Khmer sanctuary," where one could find every form of sculpture and ornament in the Khmer repertoire. The religious significance of the sanctuary doorways, through which the priests passed into the most sacred parts of the temple, made them the ideal site for iconography. These sandstone blocks became sculpted panels installed in front of the true lintel, which was supported by the main door pillars.

Depicting one of the most famous Hindu creation myths, this lintel at Phnom Rung is famous for other reasons as well: it was the subject of a celebrated dispute, having been stolen from the temple in the early 1960s. It then appeared at the Chicago Art Institute, on loan from a private collection. Successfully recovered by the Thai government in 1988, it has been restored to its original place. The scene is of Vishnu reclining on the *naga* Ananta, which floats in the primeval sea. A lotus flower grows from Vishnu's navel (vertically in this carving), and from the flower is born Brahma, who creates the world.

(above)

This lintel from Pre Rup at Angkor, completed in 961, takes some elements from the style of the previous century at Roluos, in particular the two thickly foliated branches growing sideways from the central group and the scrolled leaves hanging below. As also in earlier lintels, the middle of this one is occupied by the god Indra, seated on the head of an elephant. Indra's elephant steed is called Airavata.

(below)

A relatively unrefined but vigorous lintel at the temple of Muang Tam shows Siva sitting with his Sri on a bull. This sacred animal is Nandin, the god's *vahana*, or steed. Each major Hindu god rides a particular animal: Vishnu rides the man-bird Garuda, Indra rides an elephant, Brahma a sacred goose. The face of the demon Kala is below, a frieze of ascetics above.

Like the *makara,* the grimacing mask of the *kala*
evolved in Java, a jawless monster in one myth commanded by the gods to devour his own body, but also
linked to the eclipse. The *kala* made its first appearance in Khmer lintels at Roluos but continues to be
used today in Buddhist temples of the region. This lintel is from Muang Tam.

Ascetics commonly feature in smaller carvings, in different aspects but most often in prayer. They appear in
all phases of Khmer worship, including the Vishnuite
temple of Angkor Wat and later Buddhist temples, but
there is a special relationship with Siva, the patron of
yogis.

136

Lions were another motif that appeared in various stylized forms in Khmer architecture. Above, they occupy the carved base of pilasters framing doorways. Three-dimensional lions also appear as guardians of the entrances to temples and, as here at the Phimeanakas, at the staircases ascending pyramids. Compared with human figures and other animals such as elephants and serpents, the Khmer lions lack realism and often seem awkward, probably because the Khmer carvers had no direct experience of this animal. Lions were not part of the Cambodian fauna, and the sculptors had to rely on what they had seen of Indian, Javanese, and Chinese representations.

Colonnettes were a special feature of Khmer architecture, offering the masons another opportunity for doorway decoration. Made of sandstone, they were set on either side of the door in corners formed by the pilasters. Like the lintels, they were inherited from the earlier Chenla period. They evolved chronologically from a round section, and the typical octagonal shape had appeared by the time of the founding of Jayavarman II's kingdom. Shown at left is the entrance to the northern long annex in front of the pyramid of the Bakong, from the end of the ninth century; at right is a colonnette from the entrance to Phimai, in northeastern Thailand.

The first major attempt to build a temple-mountain was the elaborate pyramid of the Bakong in Roluos. Now maintained by Theravada Buddhist monks whose monastery is on the grounds of the original temple, it was dedicated to Siva and peaked in a single sanctuary tower, *prasat*. The present reconstructed tower replaces an earlier one of light material.

Baksei Chamkrong, at the foot of Mount Bakheng, was the first of the temple-mountains built in a durable material, brick on a stepped laterite base. It was constructed early in the tenth century, during the reign of Isanavarman II, and is one of the finest examples of a temple with a single tower. An inscription referring to Harshavarman I reads: "For the exercise of dharma and following the example of his fathers, he erected here, at the foot of Mount Indra [Mount Bakheng], golden images of two Isvaras, as well as those of Vishnu and two devis." The temple itself may have been built after these images.

In A.D. 961, south of the recently finished East Mebon and close to the southern embankment of the East Baray, Pre Rup was built. Larger and higher than East Mebon, which it closely resembles, it is a three-tiered pyramid; on top is a quincunx of towers, replicas of the five peaks of Mount Meru. Gradually, with the construction of new temples, the royal architects were edging closer to more literal, more complete representations of the cosmic mountain.

(opposite)

As in so many other areas of art, architecture, and custom, the legacy of Khmer temple towers survived elsewhere. In Thailand, the Khmer tower evolved into the *prang*, as here at the temple of Wat Phra Si Ratana Mahathat in the town of Phitsanulok. The final form of the tower at Angkor was conical, as at Angkor Wat; the Siamese developed it into a more rounded form.

145

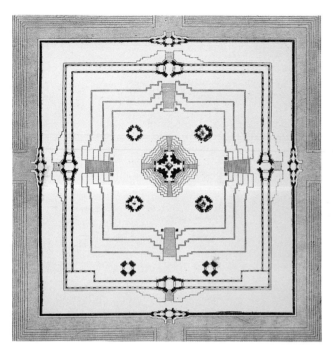

Takeo, east of the Royal Palace and just off the Avenue of Victory, was the next step toward perfection in building the cosmic mountain. Here, for the first time, the Khmer architects used sandstone throughout, and although there are signs that they were still uncertain about its treatment, this material made it possible to work on a scale befitting such an ambitious project. Surrounded by a moat (now dry), the pyramid rises to a height of over 200 feet. Begun around the turn of the eleventh century, it was completed during the reign of Suryavarman I. The plan shows the rigorous symmetry required by the symbolism. The upper terrace carrying the five towers was built in a square but set back within the overall rectangular outline of the enclosure. This elongation to the east was typical, allowing extra space within the surrounding galleries for two "libraries."

While the pyramid represented the central mountain and the concentric enclosures the *cakravala*, rings of mountain ranges, it was also necessary to symbolize the surrounding ocean. It took the form of a moat, and for the purpose it sometimes became necessary to divert the flow of the natural water supply. Few of these moats remain full of water. In this illustration from Louis Delaporte's book *Le Cambodge*, the inner moat wall is decorated by a row of mythical half-men half-birds, the *garudas* of Hindu mythology.

The *garuda*, or *krut*, as it is pronounced in Khmer, made a sudden appearance relatively late in Khmer architecture. Its origins are Hindu: it is the vehicle of Vishnu and the sworn enemy of the *nagas*, as befits a predatory bird. Once used, it appeared in a number of situations, such as high on the sanctuary tower of Phmai.

148

At the north end of the Terrace of the Elephants, *garudas* alternate with lions as caryatids to support a royal pavilion in light material that would have stood on the stone foundation. There is a religious significance even here: in the bas-relief of Angkor Wat's southern gallery, these same *garudas* support flying celestial palaces. By association, the royal pavilion is also held in the air and so compared with the palace of a god.

Although *apsaras* were an invention of Hindu mythology and appear, for instance, in the fifth- and sixth-century frescoes at Ajanta in India and at Sigiriya in Sri Lanka, the Khmers created their own version, quite different from the Indian. Not only are the features recognizably Khmer, but the frank eroticism of the Indian carvings has been turned into a more subtle allure. Further, in the original mythology the *apsaras* were always accompanied by celestial musicians, the *gandharvas*, but these were ignored by the Khmers.

The ability to deal satisfactorily with perspective remained undeveloped among the bas-relief carvers until a very late stage. They continued to have difficulty representing the feet of figures. Attempts to show them realistically led to an ugly foreshortening, and they were used very little. The common solution for *apsaras* and other divinities carved in shallow relief was equally peculiar: they were twisted to one side to present a profile. It is one of the very few imperfections in the representation of *apsaras*.

(preceding page)

Among human and divine figures used in architectural decoration, the *apsaras* were probably the greatest invention of the Khmers. According to Hindu mythology, the *apsaras* were female divinities, celestial nymphs and dancers, created for the pleasure and entertainment of the gods. Legend says they were born during the Churning of the Sea of Milk, one of the most important creation myths. Gods and demons, commanded by Vishnu, use a giant *naga* twisted around a giant pivot to churn the cosmological ocean. The ultimate goal is to produce the elixir of life, but first these nymphs emerge from the sea.

A common feature of Khmer temples was the illusion of windows and doorways on the sides and backs of sanctuaries and other buildings. These false openings underscore the fact that Khmer temples were essentially for the gods, not for congregations of the faithful. The model for the sanctuaries was the single-celled Indian shrine, intended to house a cult image to be tended by priests. In most cases, there was no need for well-lit rooms and corridors. Since the timber doors in the real entrances have long since rotted away, it is the false doors such as that above, in one of the towers of

Pre Rup, that gives the best idea of how the originals looked. A later development of false windows, which was typical of the last great period of building, under Jayavarman VII, was to carve only the lower section of the balusters. The plainly dressed stone blocks (right), as in this window at Banteay Kdei, represent a curtain blind drawn halfway. In fact, this was a device for making the carving easier and a way for the masons to be able to cope with the excessive demands of Jayavarman's construction program.

One of the most striking peculiarities that the French archaeologists discovered in a few temples at Angkor were bas-reliefs that had been completely built over, intentionally hidden from human eyes. The most accessible one lies close to the main square of the city of Angkor Thom, behind the so-called Terrace of the Leper King. As part of the cosmic symbolism of the temple architecture, the Khmers went to greater and greater lengths in successive periods to recreate Mount Meru as faithfully as possible. One element that posed obvious difficulties was the underworld. The answer here was to build it at ground level, then cover it with another bas-relief wall showing the world of human beings and some of the legendary creatures that were supposed to inhabit the lower slopes of the mountain. Henri Parmentier, who was involved in the excavation, wrote: "Behind the great carved panel, there is another one buried in the masonry, which follows all its movements; we had great difficulty in freeing it, but it revealed some carvings in a completely new state." In the photograph above, divinities of the underworld line the south face.

(opposite)
A little to the south of this terrace is the longer Terrace of the Elephants, built by Jayavarman VII. Behind the northern part, in a similar position to that of the hidden underworld behind the Terrace of the Leper King, is another hidden wall. From the iconography, however, it must have had a different purpose. The carving is an unusual deep relief and has a Buddhist motif. The central figure is this life-size five-headed horse, which can only be seen properly from three feet in front in the narrow passageway. It represents one of the forms of the compassionate Bodhisattva Lokesvara.

As it stands today, the collapsed pyramid of the Baphuon gives little indication of its early glory, for it was once the largest and most majestic temple ever built. However, in the attempt to create a cosmic mountain, a tremendous quantity of earth was used. Not enough time was allowed for the earth to settle properly before the stonework was begun, and as a result the pyramid collapsed in on itself. Now the best parts are the pavilions. The publication of Delaporte's *Voyage au Cambodge* in 1880 inspired the architect Lucien Fournerau to visit Angkor for a year in 1887. He returned to Paris to display at the salon a series of plans, elevations, and cross sections unequaled in their technique. In this reconstructed view of the Baphuon, Fournerau recaptured the grandeur of this temple-mountain when it was built in about 1060.

Angkor Wat

We look up and stand transfixed.
The great towers rise ahead,
black against a crimson band of sky.
We are within the temple precincts,
yet we still have far to go.
The causeway, broad enough for a cavalcade
of elephants, stretches on ahead.

Since May, the monsoon winds have been blowing from the southwest across the Indian Ocean and the Gulf of Thailand, and the parched land has recovered its greenness. Before dawn on this August morning the sky is slow to lighten; the heavy overcast is still black to the west and no more than a dull blue-gray to the east. We travel north from Siem Reap, along the same route that Mouhot took when he first landed from the Tonle Sap. Then it was a "dusty sandy path passing through a dense forest of stunted trees"; now it is paved and runs straight for several miles until it reaches an embankment. Directly ahead, choked with water hyacinth and barely visible in the gloom, lies a broad moat some two hundred yards wide. On the opposite bank is what looks like the edge of a forest, broken in front by a stone pavilion.

We follow the road west along the southern edge of the moat until we reach the corner, then turn north. We walk along the embankment, listening to the night's chorus of frogs and crickets. A bar of bluish mist hangs above the water to our right. By the road, the lower trunks of two *chhoeu teal* are smoldering; they are used as a source of lamp oil.

Halfway along the western edge of the moat is a terrace guarded by stone lions: it is the main entrance to the greatest of all Khmer temples, Angkor Wat. As we arrive, the sky to the right begins to change. Beneath a heavy bank of rain clouds, a deep red glow spreads just above the horizon. Dawn is the most dramatic time for visiting Angkor Wat, for it reveals the famous towers in silhouette. The sun will not shine today, but the color swelling in the distance will make an intense backdrop.

From the western terrace a causeway crosses the moat, paved with large sandstone blocks. Ahead is a long stone gallery stretching to the left and right, its line broken at intervals by pavilions and the stumps of ancillary towers. As we approach, the gallery looms higher, blocking our view of the central pyramids of the temple beyond.

We reach the entrance, a doorway in the central pavilion, and pick our way carefully through the darkness; steps and thresholds keep our eyes on the ground. At the other side is a second stone doorway, facing east. The great towers of the pyramid rise ahead, black against a crimson band of sky, a third of a mile away. The causeway, broad enough for a cavalcade of elephants, stretches on ahead.

As the sun reaches the horizon the color fades from the sky, and we hear the wind. It begins softly, growing into a rushing sound. But the air remains still; even the palm trees in the distance are motionless. What we hear is the flight of thousands of bats, wheeling through the galleries of the temple.

We start down a short flight of steps and move onto the causeway. Pools of water from last night's rainstorm reflect the morning sky. On either side, thick stone balustrades line the causeway, at intervals rearing up to become the hoods of many-headed giant cobras. These are the *nagas*, the mythical water serpents that the Khmers characteristically used in their architecture. About halfway along the causeway, steps to the left and right lead to a pair of identical buildings. Known as libraries, their original function is uncertain, but they may have been used to hold texts since they are similar to library annexes in contemporary Buddhist temples. The pages may have been strips of narrow palm leaf stacked together like slats of Venetian blinds.

Toward the end of the causeway, a short flight of steps takes us up onto a terrace that gives us a commanding view back to the west. We have been walking into a schematic version of a Hindu temple-mountain, with its concentric series of oceans and mountain ranges surrounding the five peaks of Mount Meru. So far, we have crossed an outer moat or ocean, a transverse gallery or mountain range, and a flat continent in which the libraries are something like islands. Now we are approaching the third-to-last gallery—the foothills of Mount Meru. Although our attention is really on the Meru section ahead, this grand cruciform terrace, which appears in some other temples, is a special Khmer invention. It is, in fact, so distinctive that in 1911 it prompted a professor of civil engineering from Tokyo to recall a similar feature that he had once seen on an eighteenth-century plan of an unidentified temple. When he returned to Japan he found that the plan was actually of Angkor Wat; it had been copied from a drawing made in the seventeenth century by a Japanese pilgrim, making it the earliest known plan.

The scale of Angkor Wat is so vast that it is hard to appreciate the layout without some kind of plan or aerial view. From above, the symmetry is obvious: it is a series of rectangular enclosures, one inside the next, with some additional terraces, galleries, and outbuildings. From the ground, in silhouette, the temple rises in tiers toward the center, though the corner towers on the tiers rise much higher than the long flat roofs of the tiers themselves. It is a dramatic design, though after three centuries of architecture at Angkor and Roluos, the basic form comes as no surprise. Angkor Wat is the consummate temple-mountain. The ruler who built this city-sized monument to himself was the nation's consummate king, an ambitious conqueror named Suryavarman.

The details of his accession are not known, but Suryavarman seems to have seized power after a troubled period of several years in which the rule of the country was disputed by two kings. By 1113, Suryavarman had deposed one and crushed the other, seizing the throne and unifying the kingdom. He then renewed diplomatic relations with China, began new attacks on the old enemy, the Chams, and pushed the boundaries of the empire west and north. His megalomaniacal building plans required *corvée*, unpaid labor from subjects, throughout his domain. A stone inscription in the remote mountaintop temple of Preah Vihear, about eighty-seven miles northeast of Angkor, records that in 1119 Suryavarman II gave the order "to raise the corvéable workmen of the second and third (and probably fourth) categories. They erected towers, dug basins."

His largest construction project was Angkor Wat, the monument to himself that took more than thirty years to build. His obsession with making it not only the largest but the grandest temple presented countless challenges, not the least of which was quarrying the stone in the mountains and transporting it by boat and elephant to the site. There were many design problems to be solved, from the massing of the building as a whole to the details of the bas-reliefs. Putting the horizontal elements—the walls and galleries—in the right proportion with the vertical elements—the towers rising in the center—presented difficult engineering and aesthetic questions, but in solving them, as with almost all their challenges, the builders of Angkor Wat were triumphantly successful.

We leave the view of the causeway and moat and go inside. To our left and right is the gallery containing the epic bas-reliefs, which we will visit shortly. This long, covered hallway is more than a half a mile in circumference, the boundary of the central complex of the temple. The enclosed set of galleries where we stand is a transitional area and at first difficult to understand. The next gallery-mountain ahead of us, which has slightly more than half the circumference, is twenty-

three feet higher. To link the two, the architects invented a special structure, a courtyard shaped like a
cross with a series of tiered halls. We pass through a
courtyard in the cool darkness of corbeled ceilings and
square stone columns. On each side are deep basins,
four in all; ahead is another staircase, enclosed and
dark and steeper than the last.

Emerging at the next terrace, we can see Meru for the
first time—the complete central mass of the towers. It
is as if we have emerged from the forested lower slopes
of a great mountain onto the open middle reaches. We
are standing in a courtyard bounded by more galleries;
above us, the five peaks rise too high and close to see
without straining our necks. The towers themselves are
like nothing else even in Khmer architecture and radi-
cally different from their distant ancestors, the Indian
sikharas. A few Khmer temples, such as Phimai,
Thommanon, and Banteay Samre, show the beginnings
of the curving, pointed outline, but the proportions
here are unique. They have been compared by the
many archaeologists, architects, and writers who came
here before us to cones, pine cones, bombshells, and
even pineapples. We think they look like corncobs.

We start to climb. The steps of the central tower are
the steepest of all, and they take all of our attention.
The narrowness of each step makes it easier to climb
by moving diagonally, and our eyes are on our feet.
The effect is to postpone the moment of our looking
out over the surrounding temple. As we straighten up
at the top, we can see that the staircase has carried us
above all the rooflines. The tiers of the buildings are
below us; beyond them are the moats and the straight
line of the causeway, and beyond everything else is the
forest. The view is magnificent, and the way in which
the builders have recreated the experience of climbing
a mountain is uncanny. To our left and right rise the
corner towers; galleries link the five peaks. In the middle, under the central and largest tower, is the sanctuary that once contained the sacred image dedicated to
Vishnu and the king.

It is surprisingly easy to believe that we are standing in
the exact center of the universe. A straight line extends
from our feet through the center of the rooflines, onto
the grand axis of the causeway, through the outer en-
tranceway, and off into the horizon. We are facing due
west; but almost all the other Khmer temples face east,
into the rising sun. This exceptional orientation created

a long academic debate over whether Angkor Wat was a temple or a tomb. As the direction of sunset, west has connotations of death. The tomb argument is strengthened by the layout of the famous bas-relief galleries, which we are about to visit. Half a mile of narrative bas-reliefs, four thousand square feet in all, line the galleries. They read from left to right, so that following the order of the narrative means walking counterclockwise. This direction, called *pradakshina* in Sanskrit, refers to the way a funeral procession would pass around a shrine for the dead. No grave has been found, but if that theory is true, Angkor Wat was built in part as a mausoleum for King Suryavarman II.

We reach the bas-reliefs by retracing our steps down the central pyramid and through the cross-shaped courtyard to the galleries overlooking the causeway. Turning south, we see on one side of the gallery a six-foot-high picture of intricately carved sandstone, the blocks fitted together so finely that we have to peer closely to see the joints. Ahead is the world's longest continuous expanse of bas-reliefs, all in the form of narrative sculpture. The first one, taking up this entire section as far as the corner pavilion, more than fifty yards away, is the *Mahabharata*. The narrative thread

of *The Great Epic of the Bharata Dynasty* is the feud between the Pandava and Kaurava families. A poem of one hundred thousand couplets (seven times longer than the combined *Odyssey* and *Iliad*), it is loosely based on events that took place in India between 1400 and 1000 B.C. and was written between 400 B.C. and A.D. 200, when the Vedic religion was giving way to classical Hinduism. It contains many religious asides, including Hinduism's most famous and important religious text, the *Bhagavad Gita* (*The Lord's Song*). Vishnu appears in the epic as Krishna to assist the heroes of the story, the Pandava family; since Angkor Wat is consecrated to Vishnu, the presence of the *Mahabharata* is especially appropriate.

On the right as we walk, square pillars separate the gallery from an outer hallway overlooking the distance toward the western entrance. These pillars are the architects' solution to a problem of aesthetics and weight loads, and it is a rather curious one. The gallery's corbeled vaulting only allowed for a ceiling—thus also a floor—six feet wide, which is too narrow for viewing walls hundreds of feet long. The pillars take up part of the stone roof's weight load and the outer hallway, with its corbeled ceiling and outer pillars, the rest.

(below)

A vertical aerial view reveals the concept of Angkor Wat instantly: the largest manmade model of the cosmos. The moat, some 1,400 by 1,600 yards, is the ocean surrounding the world. The concentric enclosures represent the mountain chains encircling the central continent, while the central cross locates the five linked towers, the summit of Mount Meru. From across the moat, a single line of causeways is the route from earth to Heaven. This photograph, published here for the first time, was taken during a Royal Air Force sortie in 1946. It is from a collection of five thousand aerial views made by a British officer, Major Peter Williams-Hunt, and discovered in a museum archive in 1982. The collection took eight years to process by computer enhancement.

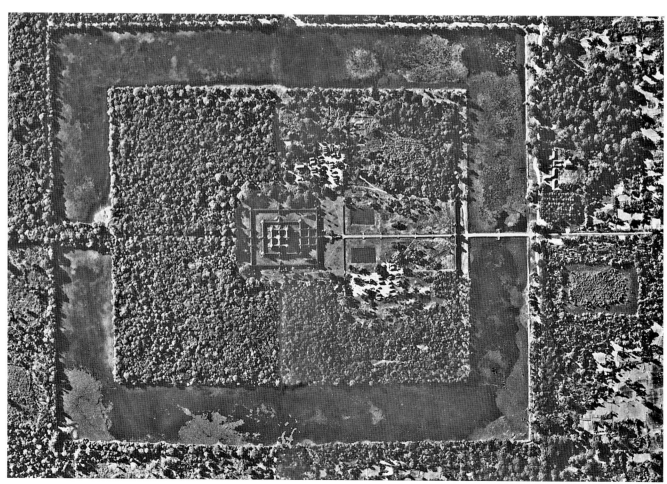

A workable but not an elegant solution, it is far bulkier than the vaults and flying buttresses of Gothic cathedrals. In practical terms, the heavier inner gallery has settled on its foundations more than the outer hallway has, causing the square pillars to crack; the French archaeologists had to reinforce the pillars with metal bands. And the diffuse light coming in from the outer hall flattens out the details of the low reliefs themselves. Furthermore, the lower walls get more light than the upper walls, which are thus harder to see. But the carvings are magnificent. In the southwest corner tower every available surface is carved, this time with scenes from the *Ramayana*, the other important Hindu epic. Around the corner is the southern gallery. It begins with a great procession under the command of King Suryavarman II, riding an elephant. Beyond another pavilion is a remarkable tableau of Heaven and Hell, in which the god of death sits in judgment over those entering from the right. The virtuous ascend to

paradise, the damned take the lower path, and by the end of the gallery, the mind is numbed by the catalogue of horrific punishments on the lower register. Paradise, which is poorly lit, receives little attention from most visitors, but Hell lives up to humanity's worst fears.

At this point we have covered almost half of the twenty-six hundred feet of bas-reliefs. If we had turned north where we started, along the western gallery, we would have seen another major theme: the final battle of the *Ramayana*, between Rama, aided by Hanuman and his monkey legions, and the demon Ravana, who has abducted Rama's wife, Sita. Along the northern gallery and the north section of the eastern gallery, the bas-reliefs are inferior; they are believed to have been executed after the completion of the temple, and the inspiration, and probably the supervision, was lacking. Rather than leave with a sense of anticlimax, we end

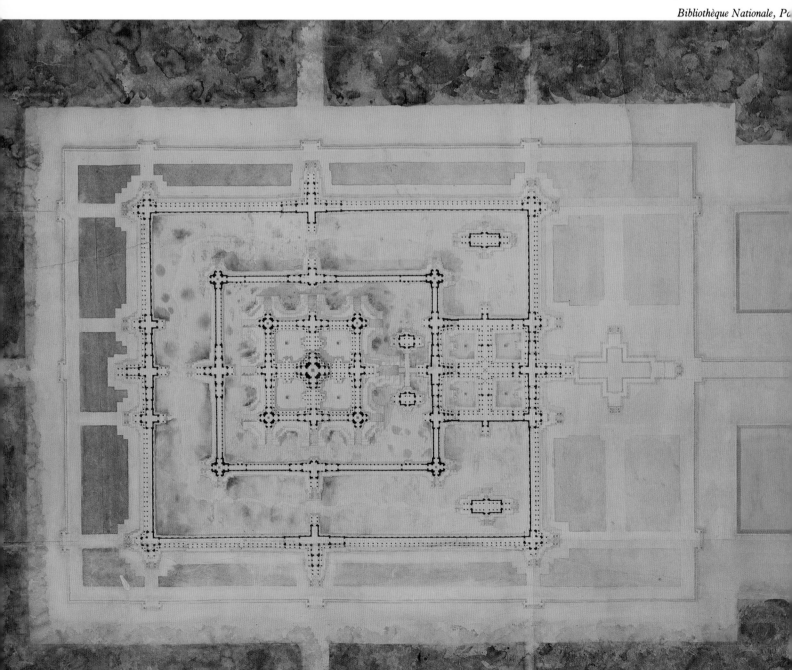

with the extraordinary section immediately around the corner, on the south side of the eastern gallery.

The Churning of the Sea of Milk is the masterpiece of the bas-reliefs. Its theme is one of the most important in Khmer mythology, the treatment is an enormous but unified tableau, and the execution is of the highest order, probably by one supremely talented artist. The body of the giant serpent Vasuki is wound around Mount Mandara, which in turn is supported on the back of a giant turtle in the Sea of Milk, the primeval ocean. In a rare instance of cooperation between gods and demons, a team of each grasps either end of the serpent's body; they pull it first in one direction and then in the other in order to rotate the mountain and churn up the sea. The idea is to release *amrita*, ambrosia, the elixir of life. In the myths, the gods and demons then fight for possession of it. Vishnu commands the two teams from the center of the composition.

Shortly before Cambodia collapsed into the civil war that ushered in the brutal regime of the Khmer Rouge, the French dismantled the roof and columns of the eastern gallery to begin restoring the temple. The fighting prevented its being put back together, so the finest bas-relief of Angkor Wat—and possibly of all Khmer art—remains open to the sky and rain. Although it is now possible to view the Churning of the Sea of Milk in better lighting than that in the remaining galleries,

the carving had been deteriorating for two decades by the time we saw it. This is all the greater pity because these gallery walls—and, indeed, the entire temple—mark the culmination of Khmer architecture. In the succession of temples begun in the early ninth century can be seen the gathering and evolution of the great themes: the temple-mountain, the recreation of the abode of the gods, the *apsaras, nagas,* and the sweeping narrative bas-reliefs. All converge at Angkor Wat; here they were realized more completely than anywhere else. After the death of Suryavarman II in about 1150 and the completion of the temple, this level of excellence was never reached again.

Nevertheless, when Chou Ta-kuan visited a century and a half after Suryavarman, Cambodia was still great. It would be another century and a half before Angkor came to an end with the abandonment of the city. As we will see, much happened between 1150 and 1431, when the temples were finally left to disintegrate.

There was one last creative resurgence of building in a new, less formal style than Angkor Wat's. It mixed elements of Hinduism and Buddhism with touches of earthy humor and even folk art. A magnificent anomaly, it combined architecture and sculpture as they have never been combined before or since. It is sad but fitting that a work of genius should be Angkor's curtain call.

The *naga*, one of the favorite motifs of Khmer architecture, here makes a startling appearance as an enormous balustrade lining the causeway that approaches the main temple across the outer enclosure. In Sanskrit, *naga* means "serpent," and the principal *naga* myths came to Cambodia from India. Sacred texts like the *Puranas* and the *Mahabharata* are full of stories of these mythical creatures, half snake, half human. Superior to man, they make up a handsome and powerful race that Brahma, the Creator, had commanded to live in an underworld called Naga-loka. Serpent princesses, of great beauty, were known as *nagi,* and more than one Indian dynasty claimed to have started through the union of these partly divine creatures with a man. Indeed, there was even a Khmer ritual in which the king had to spend the first part of each night with the daughter of the king of the *nagas.*

Serpent cults, however, were by no means exclusive to India, and it seems that the worship of snakes, as symbols of fertility and water, occurred independently in many parts of the world. Perhaps this widespread appeal accounts for the enthusiasm with which the Khmers adopted the Hindu *naga* myths. Whatever the reason, they made much more of the *naga* than the Indians ever had. Using its thick body as a balustrade was entirely a Khmer idea; the first conservator, Jean Commaille, called it "the best invention of Khmer decoration." It appears crawling along the ground at the entrance to the Bakong, but here, two and a half centuries later, it is raised on stone pillars lining the entire causeway.

The huge cobra hood of a *naga* looks over the outer enclosure from the causeway. Beyond stands one of the two isolated annexes called libraries, although there is no clear indication of their true function. The libraries are repeated twice more within the temple precincts, on the lower and second terraces, each time in pairs.

The causeway of sandstone flags runs for over 1,000 feet toward the central part of the temple from the main western entrance, here visible in the distance. Some 30 feet wide, it appears to float over the enclosure on stone pillars a little over 5 feet tall. The two libraries frame the view.

Embedded in the outer section of the causeway where it crosses the moat, two huge stone feet have been cannibalized for old repair work. They come from one of the giant figures supporting the body of a *naga* at one of the entrances to Angkor Thom.

At the end of the day, the sunlight leaves the temple in stages. Rising 213 feet above the countryside, the central tower and its four corner towers are still bathed in sunlight while the lower terraces take on the cooler tones of dusk.

In Angkor Wat, detail takes on the properties of a dimension. From a distance, the towers appear finely worked. Closer, as here in the main entrance pavilion to the enclosures, the columns and gallery roofs appear intricate in the sharp light of the setting sun; at the smallest scale, finely chiseled rosettes decorate the walls. The overall impression is of completeness, and more. Parmentier wrote: "The ornament is everywhere, even at the most invisible corners; one feels there is a homage to the god more than an attraction for the pilgrim."

After entering the body of the temple through the main entrance pavilion on the west, we reach an area of passageways and galleries running at right angles to each other. This part of Angkor Wat, known as the cross-shaped galleries, makes the transition from the lower terrace level to the second. Most of it never receives the sun. At the base of one of the columns that support the construction, an ascetic appears to be in an attitude of prayer. For the pilgrims, the most important shrine of the temple was not the sanctuary beneath the central tower but an improvised area here, where there was once an enormous, crowded collection of Buddhist statues from many places—the Thousand Buddhas. When Mouhot reached Angkor Wat, he found that "the little gallery on the right is filled with statues representing persons in the act of worshipping idols, some of these being of wood, others of stone. Many of the statues are four metres in height, and the greater number of them must be of great age, to judge from their state of dilapidation, in spite of the hardness of the stone." Today, only a handful remain, mostly headless.

In each quadrant of the cross-shaped galleries is a basin, below the passageways. These four basins, with steps leading down into them, are now dry but originally contained water for the priests' ritual ablutions. The height of the gallery walls on the side closest to the center of the temple and the depth of the basins themselves would have made them appear as dark, mysterious pools reflecting only the gray stone and the sky.

Royal Geographical Society

The tiered galleries of the cross-shaped courtyard are
an original solution to the architect's problem of linking the lower terrace to the second, which stands more
than 20 feet higher. The courtyard itself, with its four
basins (now dry), works as an enclosed architectural
unit but also rises to the upper level by means of these
superimposed stories. The stepped form of the tiers
also adds to the vertical repetition found elsewhere in
Angkor Wat.

178

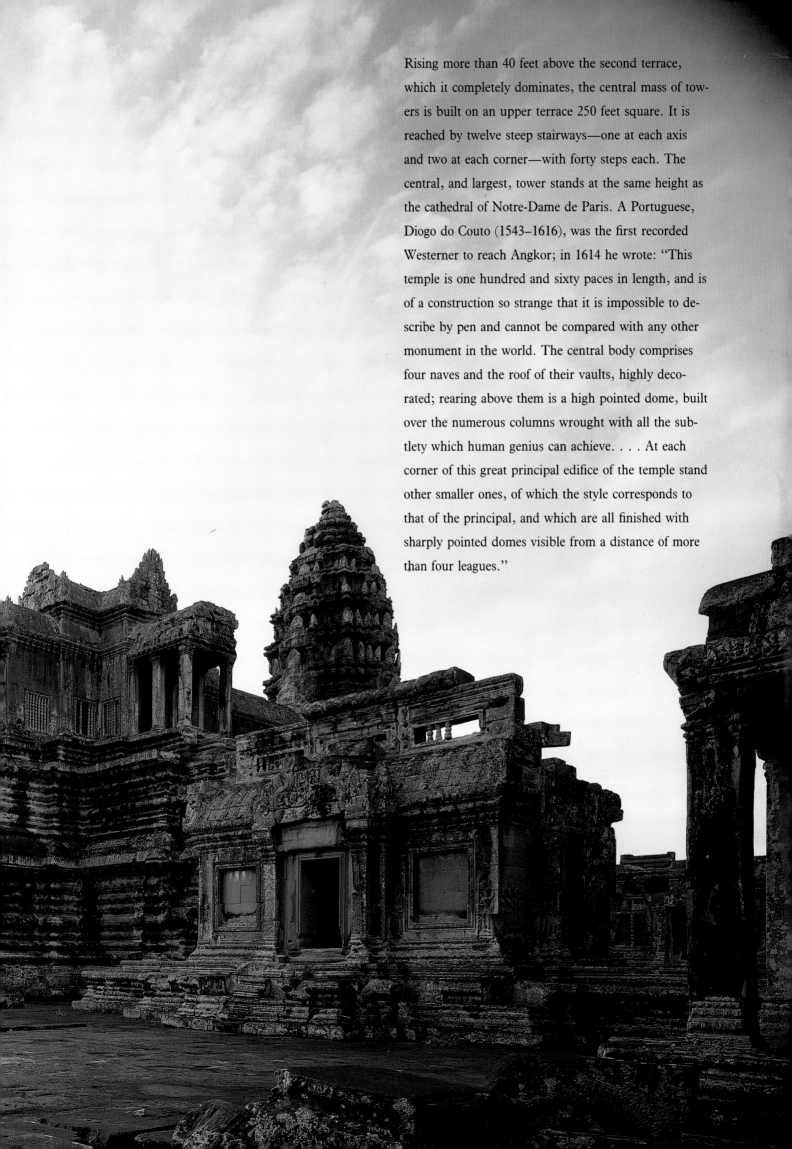

Rising more than 40 feet above the second terrace, which it completely dominates, the central mass of towers is built on an upper terrace 250 feet square. It is reached by twelve steep stairways—one at each axis and two at each corner—with forty steps each. The central, and largest, tower stands at the same height as the cathedral of Notre-Dame de Paris. A Portuguese, Diogo do Couto (1543–1616), was the first recorded Westerner to reach Angkor; in 1614 he wrote: "This temple is one hundred and sixty paces in length, and is of a construction so strange that it is impossible to describe by pen and cannot be compared with any other monument in the world. The central body comprises four naves and the roof of their vaults, highly decorated; rearing above them is a high pointed dome, built over the numerous columns wrought with all the subtlety which human genius can achieve. . . . At each corner of this great principal edifice of the temple stand other smaller ones, of which the style corresponds to that of the principal, and which are all finished with sharply pointed domes visible from a distance of more than four leagues."

The *apsaras* of Angkor Wat are its most memorable decoration. Indeed, after the five towers, *apsaras* have come to be the symbol of Khmer culture, and here they are carved at their finest. When André Malraux visited the École Française d'Extrême-Orient in 1923, Henri Parmentier gave his opinion of them. There are seventeen thousand and fifty, he told Malraux, and although "to some observers the celestial dancers seem affected and monotonous, to me they are Grace personified, the highest expression of femininity ever conceived by the human mind."

After visiting Angkor, Pierre Loti watched the palace dancers at an audience with the king in Phnom Penh. Later he wrote: "All of a sudden, the music became softer and more mysterious. One of the doors opened; into the middle of the room rushed a fantastic, adorable creature: an apsara from Angkor! It would have been impossible to create a more perfect illusion. Of the same race, she had the same features; she had the same enigmatic smile; the same lowered eyelids; the same young virgin's breasts, unfortunately veiled in silk." The tradition of the celestial dancers was reborn in the form of the Cambodian Royal Ballet, and this passed on to the Siamese court.

Another French writer, Paul Claudel, took a more jaundiced view, writing in his diary in 1921: "Everywhere these apsaras with the Ethiopian smile, dancing a kind of sinister can-can over the ruins."

(preceding page)

On a square terrace at the heart and summit of Angkor Wat, the five towers enclose the temple's principal sanctuary. It was walled up at some point around or after the abandonment of the city; when the French archaeologists began work, they discovered a deep shaft running vertically from the center. A hoard of gold objects was found here, suggesting that this shaft may have represented the axis of the universe. Lucien Fournerau, who made this elevation during his stay in 1887–88, captured the intricacy of detail of the towers and connecting galleries that is typical of the entire temple. "This decorative minuteness is pushed to the extreme; if one is struck by the work and the formidable expense represented by the ten kilometers [6.2 miles] of border in chiselled sandstone of the moats, one is no less stupefied when one thinks of the execution of the 10,000 ridge-crests which were aligned on all the ridges, so delicate that not a single entire specimen has come down to us." Henri Parmentier.

Seen from a corner of the second terrace, the northwest tower of the central group catches the last rays of the setting sun, which transforms the normally somber appearance of the gray stone. The pitch of the stone stairways up to the towers is much steeper than those from the lower levels, no doubt to reinforce the experience of the final ascent to the peak of Mount Meru. The laborious climb is a reminder of the sanctity of the center of the temple.

The central sanctuary would originally have contained the image of Siva linked to King Suryavarman II, but for centuries now Angkor Wat has been a place of pilgrimage for Theravada Buddhists, and the sanctuary today contains statues of the Buddha. Encircling it are more of the engaging, elaborately costumed *apsaras*. The jeweled diadems rising to three sharp points and the outswept curves of the dress are typical of the style of carving of the period. The hands of the countless pilgrims and visitors passed over the breasts and arms have given the sandstone a smooth, dark sheen.

(preceding page)

Returning to the main entrance of the outer galleries, we trace the half-mile of Angkor Wat's famous bas-reliefs that cover the entire surface of the galleries enclosing the temple. They read from left to right, counterclockwise, and are divided into sections that are each half of one side of a gallery. The first section, on the southern part of the western gallery, depicts a major scene from the *Mahabharata:* the Battle of Kuruksetra was fought on the plains north of Delhi between the warriors of the two clans, the Pandavas and the Kauravas. Above the ranks of the foot soldiers, commanders ride chariots; here as elsewhere in narrative bas-reliefs, the Khmer carvers have used size to represent the relative importance of the participants: the larger the figure, the greater the personage.

Attacking from the right of the 159-foot bas-relief, foot soldiers of the Pandava army and a caparisoned war elephant enter the Battle of Kuruksetra. The fine joints between the massive sandstone blocks are just visible; following an initial, lightly etched design, the carvings were made in situ after the wall was laid.

High above the windows inside Angkor Wat's south-west corner pavilion, an exquisitely carved bas-relief of the giant demon Ravana is in almost the same state as when it was carved, except for damage to one foot and ankle. Its sheltered, inaccessible position preserved it for more than eight centuries from the ravages of time and vandalism. In this scene from the *Ramayana*, the twenty-armed Ravana uses all his strength to shift Mount Kailasa, the Himalayan abode of the god Siva, back into position after an accident tipped it to one side. The sculptor has positioned the demon's multiple arms to convey a sense of movement in a way that resembles a modern stroboscopic picture.

As the bas-reliefs continue counterclockwise around the temple—the funerary direction—the southern gallery begins with a parade of the army and court of King Suryavarman II, but here he has been given his posthumous name, Paramavishnuloka, for Angkor Wat was designed to be his mausoleum. Army officers ride on horses in the parade, their rank indicated by the number of parasols above them. Daylight through the open half gallery usually shows little of the detail of the bas-reliefs; here, as with other scenes in the covered galleries, photographic studio lamps were necessary.

(opposite)

Under the command of one of Suryavarman's generals, Sri Jayasimhavarman, foot soldiers from Louvo march in orderly ranks near the head of the procession.

In contrast to the disciplined appearance of the purposeful Khmer soldiery that precedes them, a contin-gent of outlandishly dressed "barbarian" mercenaries saunter along, laughing and chatting. The inscription identifies them as "Syam Kuk," Siamese from the Menam Valley, on the edge of the empire. It was Suryavarman II himself who pushed westward and brought this region—now the heartland of modern Thailand—under Khmer control. The artist who worked on this part of the gallery took evident delight in depicting the Siamese as a clownish, undisciplined crew, but the wheel of change was already in motion: the Menam Valley was being steadily settled by immigrants from the north. A century after these figures were carved, the Siamese had declared their own independence in Sukhothai, and a century later, they were strong enough to attack, and capture, Angkor. The conquering troops who saw these bas-reliefs in the fourteenth century were able to have the last laugh.

(preceding page)

The eastern half of the southern gallery is one of the most impressive—and terrible: the final judgment of souls and their consignment to Heaven or Hell. A variety of punishments await the damned. Some are attacked by wild animals, including a tiger, fanciful giant snakes, and an accurately carved Javan rhinoceros. Quite apart from its role here, the last is of great interest, for it is now one of the rarest animals in the world; there are fewer than a hundred, nearly all in a reserve in Java.

Presiding over the bas-relief of Heaven and Hell is Yama, the Hindu god of time, immortality, and Hell. In the *Mahabharata* he is described as "crowned with a diadem, but dark and fearful with flaming eyes." The wall to his left is in three registers, but after the judgment there are just two: Paradise, set in a celestial palace held aloft by *garudas*, and Hell. The inscription that begins 218 feet of the frightful punishments that await the damned reads: "Here, the lower road is the path of Hell."

To the right of Yama, his two assessors listen to pleas for clemency but show no mercy. After summary judgment, the condemned are seized by demons and thrown down a chute that leads straight to Hell. A number of imaginative fates await them in any of the thirty-two Hells prescribed by Hindu mythology.

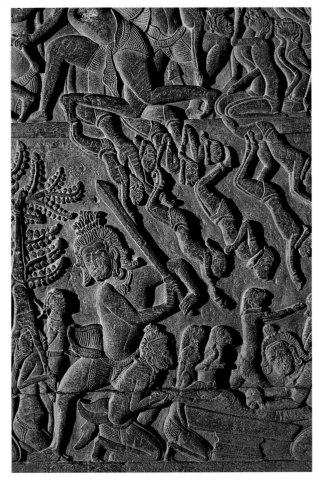

In one of the final Hells of the bas-reliefs, the damned are suspended by their hands and weighted by stones tied to their feet while nails are driven into their bodies. Heaven, on the upper register of the gallery wall, shows no such evidence of the carver's passion. Étienne Aymonier, who first described these bas-reliefs in detail, said, "The human imagination quickly reaches its limits when it comes to depicting perfect happiness. On the other hand, its resources, too often taken from surrounding reality, are infinite in the representation of the dark and saddening places of torment."

(preceding page)

With ropes through their noses, more of the wretched in Hell are pulled by a demon, who lashes out with his club. The ribs of some of the damned are etched deeply and the women have pendulous breasts, all to show their pitiful state, while the avenging demons are big and strong. These scenes have a dreadful relevance to the modern period of Pol Pot's rule, in which beatings and torture were common. Dr. Haing Ngor, whose role in the film *The Killing Fields* did much to bring the atrocities to the world's attention, describes being beaten with clubs by Khmer Rouge guards; he was starved and became very weak, but "they were strong and well fed and they were taking their exercise out on me."

In the Hell called Vaitaranidani, the Hindu equivalent of the River Styx, demons use large pincers to pull out the tongues of their victims. According to the incomplete inscription that accompanies these scenes, this Hell is for "those who follow only their criminal tendencies . . . liars . . . thieves."

On the path to Hell, the damned are pulled by ropes and clubbed; behind, an elephant takes part in the assaults. The real punishments, however, have not yet begun.

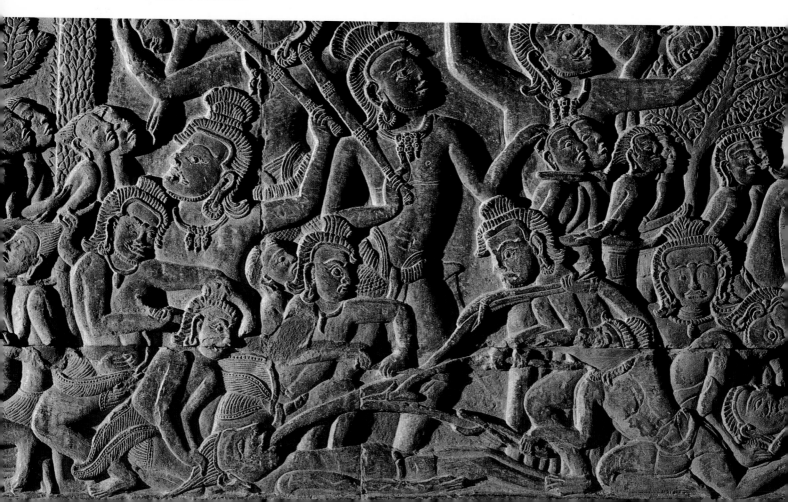

(preceding page)

There is one exception to the poor natural lighting that suffuses the galleries of bas-reliefs. In the dry season, toward the end of the day, the setting sun illuminates the lower register of the western gallery. The entire facade of the temple is bathed in golden light, which reaches the lower registers of the bas-reliefs through the open side of the half gallery. For a little over an hour, parts of the great battles of the *Ramayana* and the *Mahabharata* come alive.

In the Battle of Kuruksetra, the two armies fight in a desperate melee. The Kauravas attack from the left, the Pandavas, with pointed headdresses, from the right.

xtremity, center, and right extremity; in be-
e wall carries virtually identical lines of de-
gods. The staining is due to the bas-relief's
to the elements. Without a roof for protec-
er has penetrated the joints in the blocks, and
its only means of exit has been by leaching,
deposits to the surface of the stone.

The faces of the demons, or *asuras*, are distinctive for
their fierce expression and bulging eyes. This *asura*
stands out because of the weathering surrounding it,
evidence of recent deterioration.

The Churning was the origin of the celestial nymphs,
the *apsaras*, who were the first beings to emerge from
the sea.

The Sea of Milk

Along the southern half of the eastern gallery stretches the Churning of the Sea of Milk, a remarkable tableau of a Hindu creation myth. Vishnu presides in the center over the combined efforts of demons (at the left) and gods (on the right) to churn the cosmic ocean to produce ambrosia, the liquor of immortality. Around the pivot, supported by the giant tortoise Kurma, is wound the body of the giant *naga* Vasuki; the two teams pull the body of the *naga* alternately. There are ninety-two demons under the command of the many-headed Ravana, who features elsewhere in scenes from the *Ramayana*, and eighty-eight gods, exhorted at the far right by Hanuman. The entire bas-relief stretches for 160 feet. Shown here are the three key sections of the left e tween, th mons an exposure tion, wa in places bringing

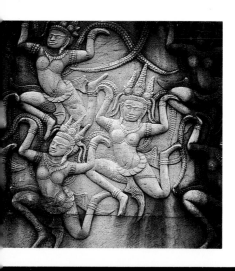

The finely carved heads of the serpent V
those of the other *nagas* in Khmer art, e
sions of the cobra. The body of this eno
wound around the central pivot of Mou
The giant tortoise under the flying figur
one of the avatars, incarnations, of the s

asuki are, like
aborated ver-
mous snake is
t Mandara.
of Vishnu is
me god.

Denizens of the deep crowd the lower levels of the
bas-relief. Close to the base of the pivot, many of the
creatures have been sliced into pieces by the violent
churning.

From the great cruciform terrace at the end of the
causeway, the western galleries, pavilion, and towers
are bathed in the clear golden light of December.

With not a single empty space, 1,076 square feet of the north wall of the west gallery are covered with the final conflict of the *Ramayana:* the Battle of Lanka. The warriors of Ravana are armed with swords, lances, javelins, and clubs. The monkeys have only stones and branches—often nothing at all. They fight bare-handed and sink their teeth into the enemy, sometimes managing to capture weapons. In Étienne Aymonier's description: "They seem overcome with fatigue but, seeing that victory is within their grasp, they keep going with renewed fervour."

Bats have inhabited Angkor Wat for centuries, but their number seems to have increased in the last two decades, with less care being taken of the temple. Corrosion from their droppings is an extra problem for the conservators. A few neighboring farmers supplement their families' diet by collecting bats as they hang during the day from the inside walls of the towers. The work is dangerous because of the overhangs during climbing, but in the impoverished state of the country in the 1980s, the bats provided valuable extra nourishment. The collector uses a hooked rod set in a bamboo handle to pull the animals out from crevices—and in doing so makes a small, if unintentional, contribution to the conservation.

The Bayon

"They had such superhuman proportions, these sculpted masks high above, that it takes some time to understand them. They smile under their great broad noses and keep their eyes half-closed. . ."

—PIERRE LOTI, *Un Pèlerin d'Angkor*

In 1177, the Khmers' ancient enemies, the Chams, launched a surprise attack on Angkor, arriving by boat on the nearby shores of the Tonle Sap. They breached the outer walls, which were merely wooden palisades, sacked the city, and killed the king. This defeat was the culmination of a decade of attacks by the Chams, who had suffered at the hands of Suryavarman II earlier in the century. The thirteenth-century Chinese writer Ma Tuan-lin described the border fighting between Cambodia and Champa in 1171: "On both sides, elephants were used for fighting, without great advantage. The [Chinese] mandarin advised the king of Champa to use horsemen armed with crossbows, to whom he taught the art of using their bows on horseback. . . . The success of the innovation was enormous; victory declared itself for Champa."

In the ensuing chaos, the eldest son of the ruler who succeeded Angkor Wat's builder saved the kingdom. Jayavarman was born sometime between 1120 and 1125 and had apparently gone into voluntary exile when his younger brother took the throne in 1160. He returned

214

when his brother was overthrown in a coup, but it was too late at that point for him to claim the kingdom. His moment came later, with the Chams' sack of the city and the death of the usurper. Gathering forces to repel the invader, Jayavarman proved to be an extremely capable military commander. His campaign, culminating in a great naval battle, was successful, and the Chams retreated. Nevertheless, it took him several years to restore order to the country, and only in 1181 was he secure enough to take the throne as Jayavarman VII.

He was about sixty years old when he came to power, and his age may have been a factor in his pressing the limits of the empire to their farthest and in his initiating a massive building program. In the area of Angkor he built the major temples of Banteay Kdei, Ta Prohm, and Preah Khan and the lesser ones of Ta Som, Neak Pean, Krol Ko, and Ta Nei. Elsewhere in the kingdom he built Banteay Chmar, Vat Nokor, and Ta Prohm of Baté. There were one hundred and two hospitals and one hundred and twenty-one pilgrims' rest houses along the major roads to Angkor. Jayavarman rebuilt the capital city itself, relocating it slightly to the north of Mount Bakheng, this time with defendable stone walls and an eight-mile moat some three hundred yards wide. The new city, although a little smaller than the first Yasodharapura, was nevertheless larger than Rome under Nero. But the building for which Jayavarman remains best known is the temple that many consider to be the most outstanding achievement of Angkor's six centuries, the Bayon.

Of all the temples, none has had such a profound effect on those who have seen it. It is an idiosyncratic mix of architecture and freestanding sculpture. The sculptures themselves are enormous stone faces with lidded eyes and thick, sensuous lips, resulting in enigmatic expressions that strike some visitors as compassionate and others as cruel. Though the faces are nearly identical, they are also omnipresent, staring out in every direction from the sides of towers rising from a terrace. Every few steps you are looking at a new set of faces, some of which are looking back at you. The Bayon is a building that interacts with its visitors.

Its appearance has changed several times. Chou Ta-kuan, writing when Angkor was a thriving metropolis, noted: "At the centre of the Kingdom rises a Golden Tower flanked by more than twenty lesser towers and several hundred stone chambers. On the eastern side is a golden bridge guarded by two lions of gold, one on each side, with eight golden Buddhas spaced along the stone chambers." By the late nineteenth century, Pierre Loti, who romanticized the ruins more than any writer, had a completely different perspective: "Through thickets of brambles and dripping lianas we had to beat a path to reach this temple. The forest enlaced it tightly all over, strangling and crushing it. Immense fig trees had rooted themselves everywhere, right up to the tops of the towers, making them serve as pedestals." The gilding was gone, probably looted before anything else.

The Bayon, in the center of Jayavarman's walled city, suffered much more collapse and decay than Angkor Wat. The latter had been maintained, more or less, by its becoming a Buddhist shrine, but no such veneration was attached to the Bayon. By the nineteenth century it was certainly hard to reach, overgrown by the thick forest. Most of the early European travelers believed it to be the royal palace; it was in such bad condition that it was extremely difficult to make any sense of the plan. In fact, the plan was inherently complicated. There is no outer wall; instead, a broad, raised esplanade forms

the approach from the east. The first enclosure is a rectangle of galleries two thousand feet in circumference; within it and above an inner rectangular gallery the enormous central mass rises abruptly. From a distance, it has the outline of a disorganized pyramid, a jumble of small towers rising in succession to a central peak. Inside, there seems to be no space to move about; it is a warren of narrow, dark passages and tiny chambers. This is how it appears today, after considerable restoration.

When the French archaeologists began their work in 1901, its state was much worse. An architect, Henri Dufour, and a photographer, Charles Carpeaux, undertook the clearing and a first survey of the Bayon. Carpeaux wrote: "Not an inch of this stone that isn't carved with an incredible richness and a charming naivety of expression. The fifty-two towers, each adorned with four colossal heads of Brahma, are capped with a tangle of creepers and even big trees. . . . You can't imagine the effect produced by these heads of Brahma, with the patina of so many centuries, covered in lichen, enveloped in creepers through which rays of sunlight still manage to filter, playing on these enormous figures and giving each a different expression: some smile, others appear sad, yet others are impassive."

The towers—actually fifty-four of them—sprouting from the corners of galleries, entrance pavilions, the upper terrace, and the central tower are each adorned with four of these faces, staring toward the four cardinal points. The Bayon's face towers are not only mysterious in the impression they create; for many years there was the mystery of who, or what, they represented.

The earliest idea was that they were the image of Brahma, the Creator in the Hindu trinity. Brahma is traditionally depicted with four faces as a sign of his omnipresence, and the Khmer religion already involved the worship of the two other gods of the trinity, Siva and Vishnu. A nearby temple built around the same time had the same faces on its gate towers and was called Ta Prohm, "Old Brahma." But the faces might also be connected with Siva. Certain *lingas*—the easily identifiable images of this god—had been discovered with faces carved on them. Perhaps, as Louis Finot suggested, the face towers were architectural versions of the sacred *linga*. Certainly *lingas* were already in some of the Bayon's chapels.

But in 1924 Henri Parmentier discovered a pediment, built over by part of the upper terrace, showing an undeniably Buddhist figure. It was Lokesvara, the compassionate *bodhisattva* from Mahayanan Buddhism. A *bodhisattva* (literally, Buddha-to-be) is one who, on the brink of full enlightenment, stops short of making the final crossing, remaining to help mankind. In 1933 a second discovery, of a large Buddha statue in a pit under the central sanctuary, confirmed the Buddhist hypothesis.

The interior of the Bayon as it is now encloses earlier monuments. What seem to be impossibly narrow corridors are actually gaps between the original walls and later structures. Parmentier described the interior: "The present space between the foundations of the central mass and the pediments over the doors of the lower gallery would not permit the handling of a sculptor's chisel nor certainly allow room for the swinging of his hammer, so that the decoration stones of the terrace have had to remain unfinished, whereas the ornamentation on the opposite side is complete. Moreover, the top paving of the terrace in some places forms a ceiling over the passageways below, and the position of these stones has sometimes destroyed the carefully executed sculptures underneath."

The Bayon was first built as a horizontal temple—like Preah Khan, Ta Prohm, and Banteay Kdei nearby—but of this plan only the outer galleries survive. An inner gallery was then built in the form of a redented cross. Sixteen small chapels connected it to the outer gallery, but all were later removed when the temple reverted to Hindu worship. The final building stage was the central massif: the principal tower and the smaller face towers, set on top of the inner galleries, which were added to at the corners to make the underlying building rectangular. The motive for all these changes is not known, but clearly at some point Jayavarman decided to do what almost every other successful king of Angkor had done—build his own version of Mount Meru. The difference was that Jayavarman was Buddhist, and the old symbolism was transferred to the newer faith.

Though the face towers dominate the experience of first visiting the Bayon, the bas-reliefs below on the outer walls are just as rewarding. The gallery walls are completely covered with carvings, the figures crammed together as if there were not enough space for the sculptors to show everything. If the artistry is not as delicate or intricate as Angkor Wat's, it is extraordinar-

ily dense in detail and event. And while the themes of Angkor Wat's galleries are grand and heroic, the outer galleries of the Bayon show, as no previous carving did, real history and everyday life.

To the left of the main entrance, along the southern section of the east gallery, the army marches to war, accompanied by its camp followers and other distractions. Men hunt birds in the trees, an oxcart has halted, and one man takes the opportunity to light a cooking fire, crouching to blow the flames. Elsewhere, too, the carvings are full of incidental details that, to a Western eye, make a refreshing change from the pomp of gods and superhumans.

It is tempting to think that this new, populist intrusion into temple carvings was a sign that the common people were at last being recognized as an integral part of

Cham warships are rowed into battle with Khmer forces.

Khmer society. The inscriptions leave no doubt that Jayavarman actually wanted to be thought of as a compassionate ruler. A stele to him reads: "He suffered more from his subjects' infirmities than from his own, for it is the people's pain that makes the pain of kings and not their own." He saw himself, certainly, as a good Buddhist. However, the basis of the Khmer empire had not changed. The temples could only be built and other massive public works could only be carried out with conscripted labor. The temples' maintenance alone involved enormous manpower, and inscription after inscription shows that entire villages were assigned to the task. The temple of Ta Prohm required the services of 3,140 villages and 79,365 people. "It is not an exaggeration to say," as Louis Finot wrote, "that, at the end of the Middle Ages, all the Cambodian peasantry was in the service of the gods; and one can think that this yoke appeared very heavy to it."

The same resource—the peasantry—was also used to fill the ranks of the army. And defense became increasingly necessary, for by the middle of the thirteenth century, the Siamese had emerged as new foes. Chou Ta-kuan remarked on Angkor's military toward the end of that century: "I have heard it said that in war with the Siamese universal military service was required," and "Only recently, during the war with Siam, whole villages have been laid waste."

The end was approaching. The Siamese attacked with increasing ferocity and increasing success. The evidence of contemporary chronicles is unreliable, but the Siamese may have taken the city more than once. What is clear is that in 1431 they captured Angkor, sacked it, and deported thousands of prisoners as slaves. Within a year, the king and court abandoned Angkor. The forest closed in.

"Decorating these walls of the Bayon are the endless bas-reliefs, the scrolls of all kinds conceived with an exuberant prodigality. There are battles, violent melees, war chariots, interminable processions of elephants, groups of apsaras, extravagantly-crowned goddesses . . . The work is more naive, less sophisticated than that at Angkor Wat, but the inspiration is more violent and riotous. And in such profusion. . . ."
Loti.

Seen through the broken doorway on top of the southern library, the towers of the Bayon catch the first rays of sunlight filtering through the trees that now cover most of the former city of Angkor Thom.

218

A *linga* dedicated to Siva stands in a mossy, dank chamber in the inner galleries; a line of corridors and similar chambers stretches beyond. In 1860 Campbell wrote: "After entering the precincts of the palace [he believed it was the king's residence] there is a labyrinth of corridors and passages of small breadth and height roofed with stone which run at right angles to one another, forming small open quadrangles by means of which light seems to have been admitted to them. These corridors although of such narrow dimensions but seemingly interminable in length must have formed the main portion of the structure; they pass at intervals into a number of small chambers leading from one to the other." The *linga,* dating from the period after Jayavarman VII's death, when the Brahman priests turned the Bayon into a place of Hindu worship, added to the early confusion among archaeologists concerning the symbolism of the temple.

220

"The monument in its present form gives a bizarre impression of accumulation and crowding . . . the structures are too close for easy circulation, and the courts are merely pits without air or light." Henri Parmentier characterized the inner galleries of the Bayon with a practiced architect's eye, realizing that the corner courtyards (above) within the inner galleries would never have been designed to be so dark and constricted. The change of plans was responsible: the courts were originally the angles of a enclosure of galleries in the shape of a cross but were later enclosed by other buildings.

Seen, unusually, from the top of a neighboring tower, the proportions of the famous face of the Bayon are quite different, emphasizing the diadem with which Lokesvara is crowned.

The state of the temple is responsible for bewildering differences in the descriptions of what would seem to be the simple matter of the number of towers and faces. Most of the fifty-four towers carry four faces, but as Osbert Sitwell wrote, "The state of dilapidation into which some have fallen renders it difficult to be precise as to the total number of them, but there are between a hundred and sixty and two hundred."

"They had such superhuman proportions, these sculpted masks high above, that it takes some time to understand them. They smile under their great broad noses and keep their eyes half-closed, with a kind of decrepit femininity. They look like the discreetly mocking faces of old women, images of gods adored in forgotten times by men about whose history we know nothing. After centuries, neither the slow encroachment of the forest nor the dissolving rains have been able to erase their expression, an ironic *bonhomie* more unsettling than the grimace of a Chinese monster."
Loti.

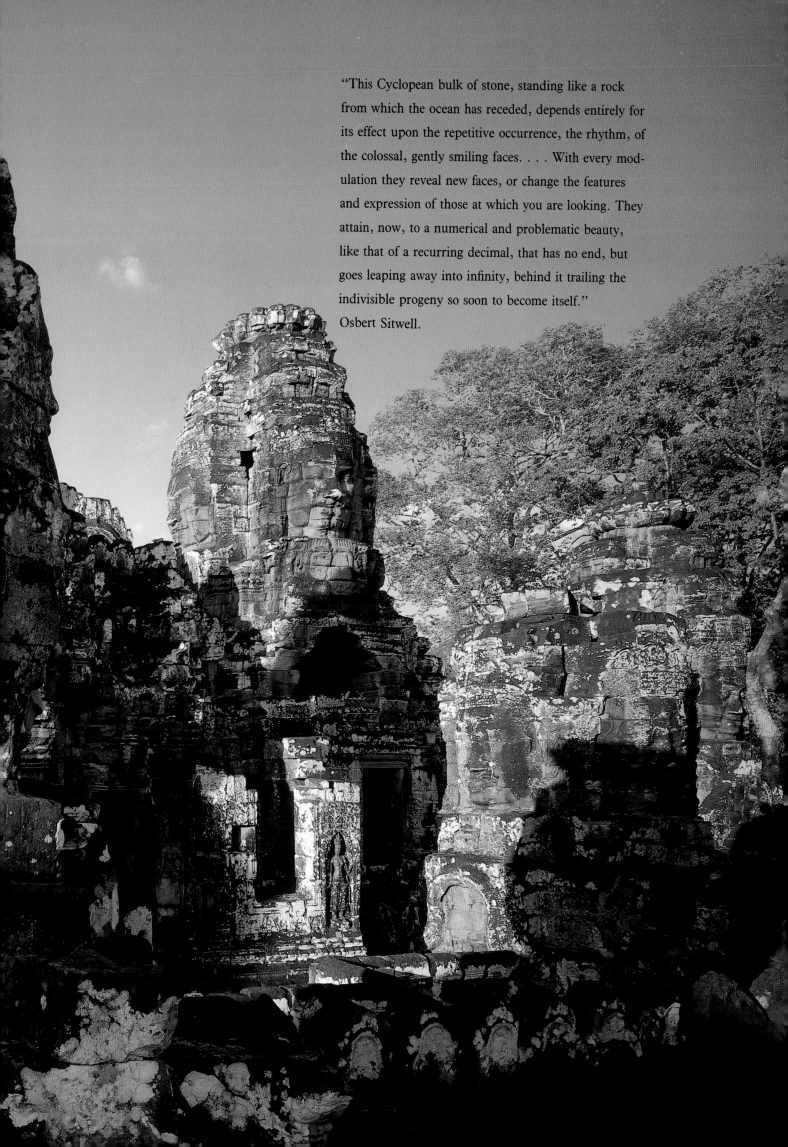

"This Cyclopean bulk of stone, standing like a rock from which the ocean has receded, depends entirely for its effect upon the repetitive occurrence, the rhythm, of the colossal, gently smiling faces. . . . With every modulation they reveal new faces, or change the features and expression of those at which you are looking. They attain, now, to a numerical and problematic beauty, like that of a recurring decimal, that has no end, but goes leaping away into infinity, behind it trailing the indivisible progeny so soon to become itself."
Osbert Sitwell.

Isolated by the rays of the early morning sun, one of
the smaller towers of the upper terrace stands apart
from the mass of the Bayon with a rare clarity. "These
towers, with their squat shapes and superimposed tiers,
bear comparison in silhouette with colossal upright fir-
cones. They are like vegetation in stone sprouting
under the sun, dense and exuberant. . . . And, from
on high, the four faces on each tower, looking out to
the cardinal points, looking everywhere from under the
same lowered eyelids with the same mixed expression
of irony and pity, the enigmatic smile. They assert,
with haunting repetition, the omnipresence of the god
of Angkor." Pierre Loti.

Even taking in the entire temple in one glance by standing outside, its structure and condition make it difficult to grasp as a piece of architecture. Henri Marchal thought it "a confused and bizarre mass, seeming to be a mountain peak that has been shaped and carved by human hands. The impression is both powerful and disconcerting. The complication of the plan of the Bayon makes it all the stranger. It is so impressive that one forgets the faults of its construction, and is entirely preoccupied by its originality. At whatever hour one walks around it, and particularly by moonlight on a clear evening, one feels as if one were visiting a temple in another world, built by alien people, whose conceptions are entirely unfamiliar."

231

The face towers "are staged and superposed in apparent disorder. One sees them surge from all sides and their strange smile animates the whole monument which, to tell the truth, resembles more the art of statuary than that of architecture." Henri Marchal.

Dancing *apsaras* are carved on the gallery columns. The style had changed significantly since the building of Angkor Wat, and the execution is more basic, with little modeling.

The *apsaras* on the outer walls of the central sanctuary, on the upper terrace of the Bayon, show a partial return to the style of Angkor Wat, with a diadem and faint smile.

Bas-reliefs of all kinds cover almost every available space in the Bayon's two galleries. The inner galleries carry mythological scenes, but the outer galleries give a glimpse of everyday life in the late twelfth and early thirteenth centuries. Here a mother plays with her children.

"For amusements, the people have cock-fights and hog-fights." This description is from the *Chinese History of the Southern Chi Dynasty,* and although it refers to fifth-century Funan, the same scenes carved on the Bayon's walls (here a fight between boars) show that little had changed.

"As in our country, drugs can be bought in the market; of these, with their strange names, I have no knowledge. There are also sorcerers who practise their arts in Cambodia. How utterly absurd!" Two common and serious illnesses at Angkor were leprosy and dysentery. Chou Ta-kuan commented that "the traveller meets many lepers along the way. . . . By some it is said that leprosy is the outcome of climatic conditions. Even one of the sovereigns fell victim to the disease, and so the people do not look on it as a disgrace. It is my humble opinion that as a rule the illness results if one takes a bath immediately after sexual intercourse—a practice which, I am told, is very prevalent here. Nine out of ten cases of dysentery end fatally."

"In Cambodia it is the women who take charge of trade. . . . Market is held every day from six o'clock until noon. There are no shops in which the merchants live; instead, they display their goods on a matting spread on the ground. Each has his allotted place. I have heard it said that the authorities collect rental for each space. In small transactions barter is carried on with rice, cereals and Chinese objects." Chou Ta-kuan.

At a halt in the march of the Khmer army, a man sets up a temporary stove by an unhitched oxcart and kneels to blow on the cooking fire. "An earthenware pot serves to cook the rice, and sometimes an earthenware stove for making sauce." Chou Ta-kuan.

Much of the daily way of life in the Cambodian countryside has persisted with little change over the centuries, despite wars and upheavals. The oxcarts shown on the walls of the Bayon at the turn of the thirteenth century are the same as those used today. A farmer rides his team by the gate tower of Banteay Kdei, one of the many temples built during the reign of Jayavarman VII and carrying his face in stone.

238

Preah Khan, called Jayasri in 1191 and dedicated to the king's father, was one of the largest temples built in the massive construction program undertaken by Jayavarman VII. Here, as in the other monuments of the period (except in the Bayon), there was no attempt to create a temple-mountain, and the plan was flat. Considerable attention was paid to the approaches, which began with an avenue lined with carved stone boundary posts.

Jayavarman's architects also completed the work
around the main square of the city, north of the Bayon.
The Terrace of the Elephants belongs to the last period
of great Khmer architecture, for after the death of Jayavarman VII little else was attempted. The terrace faces
the Royal Palace, and three staircase projections lead
onto the plaza. They are flanked by a motif that was
used elsewhere during the period: elephants uprooting
lotuses with their trunks.

Banteay Kdei, 2 miles directly east of Angkor Thom's southeast corner, was built early in the reign of Jayavarman VII. Its foundation stele is missing, and so there is no certainty even of the temple's original name, but it is possible that it is the Purvatathagata, meaning "Buddha of the East," mentioned in the inscription of Preah Khan. The stones of the central group of buildings show evidence of the hasty, rather crude construction typical of the period.

Chou Ta-kuan described the entrance to Angkor Thom: "Flanking the causeways on each side are fifty-four divinities resembling war-lords in stone, huge and terrifying." The five gates to the city of Angkor Thom—one at each axis and the last on the eastern side, directly opposite the Royal Palace—were linked to the Bayon by symbolism. The architects took the old theme of the Churning of the Sea of Milk and reworked it in massive sculpture. On either side of the approach to each gate, giant *nagas* were pulled by demons and gods. The *nagas* face outward, and the pivot for the Churning,

Mount Mandara, can only have been the Bayon itself, the cosmic symbolism of which extends to embrace the entire city. This also explains why the Bayon, of all major temples, has no enclosing outer wall; the city wall serves this function. Extra symbolism may well be loaded even on top of this explanation, for the *naga* is also compared with the rainbow, which is the Hindu bridge between the world of human beings and gods. If so, entering the city across the *naga*-lined bridge would be the equivalent of crossing into Heaven.

244

The southern gate tower is the principal route for entering Angkor Thom from Siem Reap and Angkor Wat. "The fifty-four divinities grasp the serpents with their hands, seemingly to prevent their escape. Above each gate are grouped five gigantic heads of Buddha, four of them facing the cardinal points of the compass; the fifth head, brilliant with gold, holds a central position. On each side of the gates are elephants, carved in stone. . . . Dogs are forbidden entrance, as are criminals whose toes have been cut off." Chou Ta-kuan.

"Nothing is more elegant nor, at the same time, more majestic than the monumental gates giving access to the city of Angkor Thom. They are of perfect conception and the artist who designed them holds equal rank with the prodigious decorators of Thebes and Memphis. But their construction is as defective as their distribution is excellent: the stones are falling one by one; the walls, built with vertical trenches, are at the mercy of the least shaking of a soil mined by torrential rains; lianas slowly accomplish their work of dislocation." Jean Commaille.

Afterword

"Bright red blood that covers towns and plains
of Cambodia, our motherland
Sublime blood of workers and peasants,
Sublime blood of revolutionary men and women fighters!
The blood, changing into unrelenting hatred . . .
Frees us from tyranny!
Long live, long live, glorious April 17th!
Glorious victory with greater significance
Than the age of Angkor Wat!"

—From the Khmer Rouge national anthem

To visit Angkor in 1989 was to capture something of the experience of the nineteenth-century travelers. Nineteen years had gone by since the war had reached the temples, and a decade since the end of the Khmer Rouge regime. In this short time, the forest had made a good start at reclaiming a number of the temples. Preah Khan, Banteay Kdei, Ta Prohm, Ta Keo, and some others were covered by a mantle of green. Angkor Wat continued to attract pilgrims, just as when Mouhot was here, and had regained its resident monks (the practice of Buddhism had been permitted to resume); but the outlying temples were deserted. Some halfhearted attempts had been made to clear the mines, but it was still too dangerous simply to wander about.

Occasionally an aircraft would arrive from Phnom Penh with tourists or official visitors. They would tour Angkor Wat and the Bayon for a few hours, then leave. The other temples are dominated by rural quiet. Birds chitter from the treetops. Peasants drive by in oxcarts, like living replicas of sandstone tableaux.

The background to this period of stagnation was the newest cycle of violence in Cambodia's troubled history. The scale was appalling, but many of the ingredients were traditional: ambitious despots, ruinous wars, the same foreign enemies under new names: the Chams now called Vietnamese, the Siamese now Thai. And underneath it all lay the age-old struggle to control water, to produce rice, to elevate the country above a subsistence level.

Granted, the cycle also had modern ingredients. Weapons from outside nations vastly inflated the scale of the fighting, and an imported doctrine, Marxism, added to the novelty—although Hinduism and Buddhism had once been imported, too.

In March 1970, while the nation's leader, the neutralist Prince Sihanouk, was out of the country, the rightist general Lon Nol mounted a coup and took over the government. Within days, units of communist Khmer Rouge, "red Khmer," guerrillas started to move into the temples. Sihanouk joined the Khmer Rouge and the fighting began. The following month, Henri Marchal, one of the great conservators, died of old age at Siem Reap. Bernard-Philippe Groslier, the last French

249

conservator, continued his work as best he could, but the front line stabilized halfway between the temples and the town. For a while both sides, the government troops and the Khmer Rouge, recognized the importance of the ongoing conservation: Groslier and his assistant cycled to the temples twice a week to inspect the work and to pay the laborers. But the situation continued to deteriorate. Some of the best sculptures still at the Conservancy warehouses were hidden in a concrete bunker, and the archaeologists left.

Gradually, the Khmer Rouge surrounded Siem Reap. They placed rocket launchers on Mount Bakheng, the center of the first city at Angkor; and the airport, which lay within the rockets' range, was abandoned. On April 17, 1975, the inhabitants of Siem Reap heard the Buddhist patriarch on national radio saying that the war was over and that everyone should stay quietly in their homes. The Khmer Rouge had finally taken the capital, Phnom Penh. Now they entered Siem Reap and, slowly and secretly at first, the killings began. It is now widely known that the Khmer Rouge regime, led by the infamous Pol Pot, was the world's worst government since Hitler's. What is less well known is that the Khmer Rouge were, in a sense, trying to duplicate aspects of the kingdom of Angkor. Under their flag—with its gold foreground of Angkor Wat's towers against a red background—they conscripted the people and set them to digging canals and building dams. One of their announced goals was the production of three or four rice crops a year, as their forebears had done, to build up a food surplus. They failed. Fanatical anti-modernists, the Khmer Rouge wrecked potentially useful tractors and heavy machines and executed trained engineers who could have drawn up plans. The new waterworks never approached the size or sophistication of the ancient system of canals and *barays,* and most were obliterated within years by rain and floods.

Like Siva on a rampage, the Khmer Rouge seemed to prefer destruction and chaos to the stability represented by Vishnu. They didn't build anything to last. Khmer Rouge architecture, if it can be called that, consisted of primitive thatch-roofed structures with wooden posts supporting the roofs and no walls. That was all. So much for their "glorious victory with greater significance than the age of Angkor Wat."

Somehow the ancient temples survived. The apocalyptic battles rumored to have raged through Angkor never took place (though skirmishes had). After their

250

takeover, the Khmer Rouge never unleashed their full destructive fury on the stone monuments or on the exquisite archaeological museum in Phnom Penh. They seemed to recognize that Angkor represented their own heritage.

Their soldiers wrecked most contemporary Buddhist temples throughout the country as part of an attempt to wipe out religion. They also vandalized some Angkorian statues—especially those of the Buddha—and used some *apsaras* for target practice. They wrecked the crane that was being used in rebuilding the Baphuon and treated the architectural plans at the Conservancy as paper for rolling cigarettes. But they did not break the stone of Angkor into rubble, and for them that was something like good behavior.

Theft was another matter. Western interest in Khmer sculpture rose as pieces—mostly heads, which are easier to carry—began to cross clandestinely into Thailand. After the Vietnamese invaded in December 1978 and overthrew the Khmer Rouge regime, anarchy prevailed and the sculpture trade on the black market flourished. We met more than twenty convicts who had been caught stealing from the temples and who were serving between six and ten years in Siem Reap prison. They were by no means the first thieves. The tradition of looting goes back to the sacking of Angkor by the Thais, who removed many statues before 1432. (Some of them were later taken by *their* conquerors, the Burmese, in 1569, eventually ending up in Mandalay.) In 1873 Delaporte unashamedly removed many of the finest statues for the cultural enrichment of France. And in 1923 André Malraux, author of *La Condition Humaine* (*Man's Fate*) and later the minister of informa-

tion in de Gaulle's first postwar administration, attempted to steal bas-reliefs from Banteay Srei. He was caught and tried but avoided imprisonment.

Not so the hapless thieves we met. They had stood to gain somewhere between ten and fifty dollars for a head; the real profits would be made in Bangkok, London, and New York. So eager were some looters that they were not always too careful about what they were stealing. Before the Khmer Rouge era, there had been an attempt to remove the head of a famous statue known as the Leper King. For safety, the statue was replaced with a concrete copy, but even its head was taken, reinforcing rods and all.

But the most damage was done by nature. The French conservators had identified the major problems long ago. The sand used by the Khmer builders to make a level foundation for the temples had, in the long run, only aggravated the subsidence and allowed water seepage. The sandstone itself, so amenable to delicate sculpture, had become friable with age, and in some of the reconstructed monuments the reassembled stones were unable to withstand the new pressures. In many places, structures had to be supported with concrete beams.

To these structural problems were added the renewed attacks of the strangler figs, the ceibas, and the various microorganisms that cause the stones' "skin disease." The bats returned in force, their droppings corroding the inner walls. And, just days after our first visit, a gratuitous freak of the weather created more havoc. In the worst storm since Angkor's rediscovery, hundreds of trees were felled, destroying almost three hundred and thirty feet of enclosure wall at Ta Prohm, breaking a lintel at the entrance to Preah Palilay, and more.

We returned at the start of the dry season, four months later. On the first morning we waited in the courtyard of Angkor Wat's second terrace for the rising sun to strike the central towers. A slight shiver made the spirit level on the camera tremble as a faint bass thud echoed around the galleries. This sound was repeated every few seconds; it came from an artillery engagement somewhere to the north. The next day, in the late afternoon, we were at the top of the pyramid of Takeo when a closer artillery barrage started. Only five miles away, it was in response to the ambush of a convoy on the road to the temple site of Banteay Srei. This time the Khmer Rouge was the attacking guerrillas, and the defending government a Vietnamese ally. Keeping track of the factions in Cambodia can be complicated— but the essential fact was, the fighting was returning.

Uncertainty has become the status quo in Cambodia, and the new civil war did not prevent the Conservancy, now administered by the Cambodians, from collecting sculptures strewn around the forests and clearing away the vegetation. Hundreds of workers carefully cut back the creepers and bushes, taking great pains not to damage the stone. In a short time, what had appeared to be overgrown ruins began to look more like comprehensible temples.

251

Another overgrowth, however, concealed something terrible. The road from Siem Reap to Angkor Wat runs straight north from the faded Grand Hotel. About midway, near the Welcome sign and set back about one hundred yards on the left, stand the remains of a Chinese school. In 1970 the school had been on the front lines between the Khmer Rouge and the Lon Nol government troops. By the time of our visit, most of the trenches from that era were covered with grass and beginning to blend back into the landscape, but near the Chinese school the trenches had been excavated when human bones were found. Here, within sight of the glorious towers of Angkor Wat, the Khmer Rouge had made a killing field. The wrecked school building,

its floor covered with cattle dung, now contained a low wooden platform bearing a few hundred skulls and some blindfolds. The horror unleashed here echoed the punishments of Hell in Angkor Wat's famous south gallery.

For the temples of Angkor there seems to be hope, however uncertain the future of the country. Even as the Vietnamese troops occupied the country, the restoration of Angkor Wat began again, this time supervised by Indian archaeologists. India was the first country outside the Soviet bloc to recognize the government installed by the Vietnamese, and in the dry season of 1986–87 it embarked on a six-year program to clean and restore the principal monument with an army of Cambodian workers. The first step was cleaning, but the program has been controversial, mainly because of some of the chemicals used to treat the stone. More recently, other organizations have begun to assess the state of the monuments and to plan restoration projects. None of them will be too soon. To the casual eye the stone of Angkor may seem permanent, but it has only lasted longer than its builders. These great temples to the Hindu gods are at the mercy of the ultimate destroyer named in the *Mahabharata:* "Time ripens the creatures, Time rots them."

GLOSSARY

Acroter   A pinnacle or other ornament that stands on a parapet.

Airavata   A triple elephant, the mount or vehicle of Indra.

Amrita   The elixir of life, or ambrosia, produced by the Churning of the Sea of Milk, over which the gods and demons fought.

Anastylosis   Integral restoration.

Apsaras   Celestial dancers who entertain the gods and are the sensual rewards of kings and heroes who die bravely. In Hindu mythology they always performed with the celestial musicians, gandharvas, but in Khmer mythology they were elevated alone to special importance in temple decoration.

Asura   A demon.

Avalokitesvara   The Compassionate Bodhisattva, also known as Lokesvara.

Avatar   The incarnation of a god in the form of a human or animal. Rama is one of the avatars of Vishnu.

Bali   The brother of the monkey-king Surgriva, who usurped the latter's throne in the Ramayana epic.

Baluster   A circular post or pillar, used in a barred window or as the upright of a balustrade.

Balustrade   A railing in which the upright members are balusters that are covered by a beam or coping.

Baray   An artificial lake or reservoir.

Bodhisattva   In Mahayana Buddhism, a being who voluntarily stops short of reaching Buddhahood in order to help humanity.

Brahma   The Creator of all things.

Brahman, Brahmin   A Hindu priest.

Cakravala   The concentric rings of mountain ranges that enclose the world mountain Meru in Hindu cosmology.

Chenla   The Chinese name for Cambodia before the Khmer era.

Colonette   A small, usually decorative column in Khmer architecture which stands at either side of a doorway.

Corbel   A deeply embedded load-bearing stone projecting from a wall.

Corbel arch   A false arch built from corbels projecting from opposite walls in tiers so that the topmost stones meet in the center.

Cornice   A decorated projection that crowns or protects an architectural feature such as a doorway.

Dvarapala   A temple guardian, normally sculpted as a watchman at a door.

Fronton   The triangular vertical face used decoratively above a lintel or over a portico or other entrance.

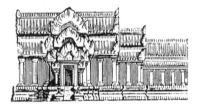

Funan   The oldest Indianized state of Indochina and the precursor of Chenla.

Ganesh   The elephant-headed son of Siva.

Garuda   A mythical bird-man, the vehicle of Vishnu.

Gopura   An entrance pavilion surmounted by a tower.

Hamsa   A sacred goose, the vehicle of Brahma. In Buddhism, it represents the flight of the doctrine.

Hanuman   The monkey-general and ally of Rama in the Ramayana.

Hara   Another name for Siva.

Hari   Another name for Vishnu.

Harihara   The god combining Siva and Vishnu in one image.

Harivamsa   The sacred book containing the genealogy of Hari, that is, Vishnu.

Hinayana   "Lesser Vehicle," referring to the traditional, conservative form of Buddhism, which concentrates on the doctrine rather than on the worship of the Buddha or Bodhisattvas. Its adherents use the term Theravada instead.

Indra   The Vedic god of the sky, clouds, and monsoon.

Isvara, -esvara   Lord, supreme deity.

Kala   A motif adopted from India; a demon commanded to devour itself. It is commonly sculpted as a guardian over a temple entrance.

Krishna   One of the incarnations of Vishnu.

Krut   The Cambodian name for garuda.

Laterite   A red, porous, iron-bearing rock that is easy to quarry but extremely hard when dried.

Library   An isolated annex usually found in pairs on either side and in front of the main entrance to a temple or an enclosure. It is a traditional name, and there is no certainty that the libraries were actually used as repositories for books.

Linga   The stylized image of a phallus, representing the essence of the god Siva.

Lintel   A load-bearing or decorative block spanning a doorway across the two pillars.

Lokesvara   See Avalokitesvara.

Mahabharata   A major Hindu epic written between about 400 B.C. and A.D. 200. Its central narrative describes the feud between the Kaurava and Pandava dynasties.

Mahayana   "Great Vehicle," referring to the later form of Buddhism in which the Buddha and Bodhisattvas are worshiped as deities.

Makara   A sea monster with scales, claws, and a large head, often in the form of a crocodile, sometimes with the trunk of an elephant. It appears in Khmer sculpture, having come from India through Java.

Meru   The cosmic or world mountain that lies at the center of the universe of Hindu cosmology. Its summit is the home of the gods.

Mount Kailasa   The abode of Siva, named after the actual mountain Kailas in western Tibet.

Naga   A many-headed serpent with numerous mythological connections associated with water, fertility, rainbows, and creation.

Nagara   A Hindu city or capital; the origin of the Khmer word "Angkor."

Nandin   A sacred bull; the mount or vehicle of Siva.

Pancha Yatana   In Hindu religious architecture, a temple with a main central sanctuary surrounded by four other shrines that are connected to it by cloisters.

Pediment   See Fronton.

Phnom   The Khmer word for "hill" or "mount."

Pilaster   A pillar with square or rectangular sections that is actually engaged in the wall so that it becomes a projection.

Portico   An entrance porch.

Pradakshina   The clockwise (and usual) procession around a temple, keeping the shrine to the right. See also Prasavya.

Prajnaparamita   The female form of the Bodhisattva Lokesvara.

Prang   The Siamese variation on the cone-shaped Khmer tower.

Prasat   A tower-sanctuary. From the Indian prasada, a terraced pyramid temple typical of South India.

Pratibimba   The Hindu concept of making an earthly representation of a heavenly form.

Prasavya   A counterclockwise procession around a temple, keeping the shrine to the left; this direction is taken if it is a tomb. See also Pradakshina.

Preah   Sacred.

Quincunx   An arrangement of five things in which four occupy the corners and the fifth the center. See also Pancha Yatana.

Rama   One of the earthly incarnations of Vishnu and the eponymous hero of the Ramayana.

Ramayana   The major Hindu romantic epic that traces the efforts and adventures of Rama to recover his wife, Sita, who was kidnapped by the demon Ravana.

Ravana   A demon with many arms and many heads; the villain in the Ramayana.

Sikhara   A pointed tower in Indian architecture.

Sita   The wife of Rama.

Siva   One of the three major gods in Hinduism; the god of destruction but also of rebirth.

Stele   An upright slab bearing an inscription.

Stucco   A plaster used decoratively for covering walls (brick walls in Khmer architecture).

Surgriva   The monkey-king ally of Rama in the Ramayana.

Tandava   Siva's dance in which he brings the universe both to destruction and to a new beginning.

Theravada   The traditional form of Buddhism. See also Hinayana.

Trimurti   The Hindu trinity of gods: Brahma the Creator, Vishnu the Preserver, and Siva the Destroyer.

Ushnisha   The flamelike protuberance on the head of Buddha, symbolizing his all-encompassing knowledge.

Vahana   The mount or vehicle of a god. For example, Siva rides the Nandin bull.

Varman, -varman   Protégé.

Vasuki   The name of the giant naga used by the gods and demons to churn the Sea of Milk.

Vault   An arch extended in depth.

Vedas   The four religious books that instruct Brahmanic ritual. The most famous is the Rig Veda, which was composed in the first millennium B.C.

Vishnu   One of the three major Hindu gods; the preserver and protector.

Yama   The god of death.

BIBLIOGRAPHY

Aymonier, Étienne. *Le Cambodge*. Paris, 1901–3.

Becker, Elizabeth. *When the War Was Over*. New York, 1986.

Boisselier, Jean. *Le Cambodge*. Paris, 1966.

Bouillevaux, Charles-Émile. *Voyage dans l'Indochine (1848–1856)*. Paris, 1858.

Briggs, Lawrence Palmer. *The Ancient Khmer Empire*. Philadelphia, 1951.

Bulletin de l'École Française d'Extrême-Orient.

Carpeaux, Charles. *Les ruines d'Angkor, de Duong-Duong et de My-Son*. Paris, 1908.

Chou Ta-kuan. *Notes on the Customs of Cambodia*. Translated into French by Paul Pelliot. *Bulletin de l'École Française d'Extrême-Orient 1902*. The French version translated into English by J. Gilman d'Arcy Paul. Bangkok, 1967.

Claudel, Paul. *Journal*. Paris, 1921.

Coedès, George. *Les États hindouises d'Indochine et d'Indonesie*. Revised edition, 1964. *The Indianized States of Southeast Asia*. Edited by Walter F. Vella, translated by Susan Brown Cowing. Honolulu, 1968.

———. *Pour mieux comprendre Angkor*. 2nd revised edition, 1947. *Angkor: An Introduction*. Edited and translated by Emily F. Gardiner. London, 1963.

Commaille, Jean. *Guide aux ruines d'Angkor*. Paris, 1912.

Dagens, Bruno. *Angkor, la forêt de pierre*. Paris, Gallimard, 1989.

Delaporte, Louis. *Voyage au Cambodge: l'architecture Khmer*. Paris, 1880.

Faure, Élie. *Mon périple*. Paris, 1932.

Garnier, Francis. *Voyage d'exploration en Indochine*. Paris, 1873.

Glaize, Maurice. *Les Monuments du groupe d'Angkor*. Paris, 1963.

Groslier, Bernard-Philippe. *Angkor: Art and Civilization*. Translated by Eric E. Shaw. New York, 1966.

———. *Angkor: hommes et pierres*. Paris, 1964.

Jumsai, Sumet. *Naga: Cultural Origins in Siam and the West Pacific*. London, 1988.

Lewis, Norman. *A Dragon Apparent*. London, 1951.

Loti, Pierre. *Un Pèlerin d'Angkor*. Paris, 1908.

Lunet de Lajonquière. *Inventaire descriptif des monuments du Cambodge*. Paris, 1902–11.

Macdonald, Malcolm. *Angkor*. London, 1958.

Madsen, Alex. *Silk Roads: The Asian Adventures of Clara & André Malraux*. London, 1989.

Mouhot, Henri. *Diary: Travels in the Central Parts of Siam, Cambodia and Laos During the Years 1858–61*. Abridged and edited by Christopher Pym. London, 1966.

Ngor, Haing S., and Roger Warner. *Surviving the Killing Fields, A Cambodian Odyssey*. New York, 1987.

Parmentier, Henri. *Guide to Angkor*. E.K.L.I.P.

Richards, P. W. *The Tropical Rain Forest*. Cambridge, Eng., Cambridge University Press, 1966.

Robin, Simone. *Angkor*. Paris, 1948.

Rowland, Benjamin. *Art and Architecture of India*. Pelican History of Art.

Sitwell, Osbert. *Escape With Me! An Oriental Sketch-book*. London, 1939.

ACKNOWLEDGMENTS

The political conditions at the times of our visits to Cambodia made prolonged access to Angkor very difficult; the Vietnamese army was withdrawing and the civil war starting again. It would not have been possible for us to have written and photographed without the considerable help we received from many people, inside the country and out. In particular, we would like to thank the following for their generous assistance: Chum Bun Rong, Mme. Sun Saphoeun, Pich and Mak Kunaly in Phnom Penh; Leng Vy, Kossom Saroeun, Hao Sitha, Vong Vorn, and Yeang Sokhan in Siem Reap; Siriporn Buranaphan, Vicky Gregory, and Susan Walker in Bangkok; Kaori Aochi in Tokyo; Mlle. Do Lien in Ho Chi Minh City; John Sanday in Santa Monica; Sam Heath and David Hawk in New York; Jacques Dumarcay and Claude Jacques in Paris; and Don Moser and Caroline Despard in Washington, D.C.